Angel in the Mirror

Healing Traumatic Brain Injury and PTSD
Through Western Medicine and Spirituality

Keli Kane

ISBN: 978-1-916540-24-8 (paperback)
ISBN: 978-1-916540-25-5 (hardback)

Contents

Dedication

You know who you are,

Thank you for helping me rise from the ashes as a Phoenix. I hope you're proud of me. I will always be your little bulldog. I love the signs you send us ❤

About the Author

Keli is a Reading Specialist, Motivational Speaker of Overcoming Traumas, and Healer working with TVGUESTPERT. Her loving and compassionate demeanor has destined her to teach young children as a Kindergarten Reading Specialist. She has a Bachelor of Science Degree and a Master of Science in Education Degree. She is permanently certified by New York State as a Public-School Teacher Pre-Kindergarten, Kindergarten, and Grades 1-6. She is also permanently certified as a Reading Teacher in grades K-12. She has been and is currently still employed in the same school district as a Reading Specialist teaching grades K-12 since 2003. Throughout her life journey, Keli has suffered and overcome many unforeseen changes, traumas, and upheavals. Keli has used her God-given gifts to change not only her own life but others as well through energy healing. She has also studied Shamanism and became a Usui Reiki Master and Teacher.

Keli is an extremely confident woman exercising excellent self discipline to create the strength needed to overcome traumas and obstacles. She wears her heart on her sleeve and is truly as authentic as one can be. She can easily be described as an Earth Angel, always finding the best in a person or a situation. Children and animals are drawn to her white light and high vibrational energy. Keli is a true social chameleon, and those around her are at ease sharing their thoughts and feelings. Her positive energy and enthusiasm precede her entrance into a room.

Introduction

People describe me as a playful ball of positive energy. I've been told by many that my energy precedes me into rooms like a bright white light. Often stated, I have kind eyes, and when people look into them, they are also looking into a part of themselves. I'm a walking social chameleon with the gift of speaking, and anyone who needs to chat with me knows that I am a safe haven to run to for help. I'm ridiculously playful and look for any opportunity to clown around with the kids, sometimes getting all of us in trouble and apologizing for the raucous later. I wear my heart on my sleeve proudly, so everyone knows they are loved and appreciated. I'm often blowing kisses, making heart signs with my hands, or shouting, "I love you". I don't pretend to be happy, I actually enjoy and need that sensation of love and well-being like water. I love love, and I love emotional happiness. Yet there are times when trauma sneaks up, and work needs to be done to return to this state of blissful peace.

The universe has been giving me signs and synchronicities for years that I am supposed to share my deepest and darkest moments with the world. Many have told me, "one day, you're going to write a book about your life to help others," and I laughed at their extremely overly optimistic statement. I wasn't ready, and I felt like I didn't have the power or knowledge of how to help anyone, let alone myself, at the time. I have spoken with so many people about "my lifetime," calling out facts like I'm reading the narrative objectively off of one of my reports at work. The response is always the same, which is stunned silence. The look on people's faces as I share it with them, speaking with not a single drop of tears falling on my cheeks. I don't show what I've been through on the outside. At least I pride myself on being composed most days. I waited years to share my suffering and accomplishments because I needed to demonstrate to everyone that I am okay and fully functional with an occasional trip up because I have lost so much in such a short period of time. Now that I've earned that right to speak, it's time to stand up and be a role model. Stating that I could even serve as a role model is difficult for me to say because, internally, at times, I struggle as a humble soul working diligently to remain grounded with a happy spirit. This gets in my way, sometimes keeping me from stepping out of my comfort zone. Questioning why I would even be so important is the overthinking thought that runs rampant in my mind when I try to gain the courage to share these events. It's still difficult because you cannot control everyone's perceptions or opinions. It's theirs to use at their own discretion, and that fear is what held me back for years. I'm no longer hiding.

It was only in this past year that some things truly broke me emotionally to a returning point of despair and feeling of drowning in problems that have been approaching in the rear view mirror for a period of time. The chaos finally caught up to me to be dealt with in a vengeance. There were so many obstacles that I had to overcome that I had no choice but to prioritize which problem was worse than the other, all of them being time sensitive. While fighting to solve one battle, I was already preemptively planning how to fix the next situation before it became its worst. To keep myself in good spirits, I was doing everything I was trained to do in order to keep myself free of depression to the best of my ability each day. Fighting off the fear of judgment, I started sharing videos of my experiences and the healing knowledge that I had to offer. It was quite the experience developing social media platforms on Instagram and Twitter, and then TikTok videos began after advice was given to me to do so from my friend Cristina. I have a journey to help others which is the priority canceling out my fear of judgment and the unknown. The video creations worked, and as I clumsily navigated my way through the initial push-backs from peoples' frames of mind, it got easier to shine the light of who I truly am. It's only now in the year 2023 that I am finally in a place of security and free of these obstacles to have the capacity to look back at all of these traumas sharing how I weaved in and out of the light and darkness. The bottom of your heart can be the darkest place, and when you're there, you better hope that you learn to become your own light. That's exactly what I did to not just survive but ascend and transform. It's not good enough to just survive. You have to live! I studied the light and the darkness to find my own personal ying/yang. I learned how to alchemize the pain and turn it into power.

Some of these chapters are going to show the true depth of how dark it was emotionally. I timidly share it because I am a Reading Specialist who specializes in working with children. I'm successful in my 20-year career as Reading Specialist and didn't want anyone doubting my abilities to continue my career safely while fighting extreme amounts of depression from the traumas at hand. Demonstrating strength for the past eight, almost nine years after this accident and traumas, adds truth to my story of recovery. If I had written this any earlier, I would not have had the full story to share, and a partial story simply would not have its full healing potential for others. I'm a freely open and vulnerable person with a compassionate soul. My desire to share this demonstrates my vulnerability in order to help people navigate from the darkness back into the healing light.

This was initially a book about how to survive a brain injury. I was struck by a drunk driver on June 7, 2014, at 10:42 AM on a Saturday morning. It was supposed to be about the recovery process, struggling with PTSD, the way the law processed my case, medications taken, the doctors and specialists that saved my life, and just in general, how to navigate such a difficult experience. I have also undergone a spiritual elevation as well. I'd say "awakening," but I have always been a gifted individual. I kept my gift hidden during my life, only sharing it with individuals who were around me who had no choice but to question how or why I was able to see, hear, feel, smell, and know certain things. How can I explain healing so well without explaining the spiritual work and healing I did with a Pastor, Shaman, Reiki Master, beautiful White Witch, and my gifted medium friends? This accident led me to find my soul tribe around the world.

The accident was only the first part of my trauma, believe it or not. Yes, I had already suffered some childhood traumas, and I was unsure whether or not I was even going to share them. I do think it's relevant because I already had cracks in my emotional foundation before being hit with the succession of traumas after the brain injury.

Following the auto-accident after years of healing work was another trauma. While I was healing, it was challenging to get back and forth to my parents as much, and I suffered an extreme loss of time to spend with them. Their health declined during this time. The Pandemic hit, and COVID delivered its challenge to teach virtually to Kindergarten students. While this was happening, my parents were in and out of the hospital many times, also in a nursing home, without visitation rights. The only communications we had were through phone, Facetime when they could actually figure out how to use it, and seeing them through literal glass windows. These were the last moments we had with them. We removed our father from the nursing home and brought our mother home for Home Hospice care. No one, and I mean not a single soul, could have prepared us for what was about to happen. The whole process of Home Hospice is kept to a bare minimum, and I believe that it is done on purpose not to traumatize family members before the actions take place. My father slipped and fatally hit his head and passed away in his own home alone on the 11th day of Hospice care while we were taking care of our mother. We were instant orphans in 36 hours. They died on June 14 and June 16, 2020. After that tragedy, I got a separation in January 2021, with the divorce finalized in June 2021. I then had to sell my home that I had lived in for 16.5 years and move into an apartment with my son, who is now age 15.

The most prominent delay in writing this book is the actual trauma itself, revisiting the darkest places that I managed to escape mentally. I would write something and be proud that I was able to get it out to the world. Later I would review what I wrote in an attempt to move forward in writing and get so traumatized by the details that I again would have to walk away and calm myself. Getting to this point where I am actually typing a "forward" is ground breaking. Not many know that I am trying to complete this book. I have mentioned it so many times and have delayed it so long that I have no choice but to just complete the task and heal myself in the hopes of also healing others. This was brought up in a discussion recently with my psychologist Dr. Mark Hammel, Ph.D. We realize the challenges. However, the benefits of guiding people, where they can find help or navigate the process, far exceed my insecurities. This is not an easy task to put your life and experiences out into the world. I have a bigger spiritual path, and it does not include my own fears. I'm doing what I am called to do, and that is to be a healer. I'm sharing my traumas and what I did to survive and be happy in hopes that you, too, can find the courage and strength to carry on and not just be alive but to truly live. Truly live in the movement because not a single moment is promised. Here is my attempt to share this incredibly difficult journey of healing to become my own Angel in the Mirror.

Chapter 1

I've replayed the scenario in my head too many times about the accident that day on June 7, 2014. I'll do my best to give as vivid a picture as I possibly can, but almost nine years have passed, and I did have a brain injury, being deemed "mentally disabled" for over a year. I'm managing this from my own memories, my family conversations, the documentation I kept, and the journaling that I took while this was all unfolding in 2014.

My schedule had changed that day, and I was never the one to drop my son off at baseball on Saturday mornings. My son was only seven years old at the time. I distinctly recall hurriedly running around getting gift cards to make sure I had the retirement gifts for the teachers I was going to see later that evening. I had collected money for them and was in a mad rush to get everything done. I was already in a heightened rushing state to "accomplish tasks" and get it all done "perfectly". I'll explain later how this accident has changed everything about the way I operate in comparison to this "pre-accident Keli". I was the frantic Mom who was trying to get it all together and complete tasks, rushing, calling out to my son to get dressed and put his cleats on. It was 10:35, and he was supposed to be on the field at 10:30. The field was only 2 minutes from our home at the time. When we arrived at the field, he got out of the car and started running to the field when I noticed he had his Nikes on and not his baseball cleats. I was upset and frustrated and yelled, "why didn't you put your cleats on when I asked you to"? I told him to go on the field, and I would run home and get them. I was panicking. In hindsight the truth is I should have been wondering what in the world I was panicking about. I just felt like I never fit in this small hometown area that I didn't grow up in where "everybody knows your name"- yes, that's a song reference to Cheers. I have to write with my true personality, and I quite often break out into songs to relay my points. It's the hidden entertainer in me.

I didn't want to be judged as the "bad Mom". What would have been the problem if a seven-year-old played in his sneakers one day? I saw his grandfather in the stands and motioned to watch my son. I stood there with my hand on the door handle with this deep gut feeling that screamed, "Let it go. Don't leave. Let it go". However, I didn't listen to my intuition, guides, angels, and ancestors. I got in the car and made it to the house in two minutes.

After grabbing the cleats, I was again drawn to pull the car over to the side of the road near a church where they were having a raffle on a riding lawnmower. None of you needs to know that information; however, it is relevant because my spiritual team was desperately "holding me" twice, and I was only partially listening. I got back into the car, and it was now 10:42 AM. The sun was shining, and it couldn't have been more of a beautifully comfortable climate. I passed the church on the left and had a 90-degree turn where the roads just wind blindly to the left, and I mean blindly. There are brushes there on the left at the corner, and you see nothing past them as you bravely make that curve. (Side note: we have a corner just like this as the final turn to get to my elementary school where I teach, and it scares me all the time. The brushes protrude, and despite the town's amazing attempt to keep it clear, it overgrows quickly. It's a constant trigger that I battle each day, both in my hometown and where I teach.

The right side is a wall of stone and a cliff that drops straight down with roads going to the Hudson River. Angelically the accident took place on the corner of Church and Hill Street. I never had a chance to maneuver away from this drunk driver. There was absolutely no vision and not even a thought in my mind that while I moved forward, a car would drive directly into me, t-boning me in the driver's side at 30 mph. My car was only going around 5-10 mph to take that corner, so I was basically just a sitting target for this extremely drunk driver. As an afterthought, and wishing that it never happened in the first place, I can say that I don't believe "seeing it coming" or "bracing myself" would have made a positive impact. The damage may or may not be the same, but I don't want to replay seeing a car driving into me ever. I have enough residuals from this accident. I am glad that part of this trauma isn't compiled along with the rest of it.

I have been asked repeatedly to tell this story to what seemed a million times being grilled by doctors, lawyers, insurance companies, and people in general involved in this situation. My story remains the same because it is the truth. I do not pretend to know every single detail, how could I because clearly I was unconscious for a portion of time, and no one has ever been able to tell me how long or what I even hit my head on? They asked me when I was the one unconscious person in the car, which is baffling. I do not remember the initial impact at all. The car companies, like OnStar, should invent a camera that only records "on impact". This would at least settle the "what happened after the impact," which is what you are grilled on for years after the accident over and over and over and over again. That repetition was done on purpose because that is the only way for me to demonstrate briefly what it's like when giant insurance companies and lawyers get involved. Adding on that, friends and families of certain people of "status" and professions unleash another level of unnecessary pressure when all you are trying to do is heal so you can live your life. I was trying to finish my teaching career, which I still owe

$78K for. (Side note, I have been working for years to clear that loan. They were government loans, and I have taught for 20 years in a qualifying school for "teacher loan forgiveness", and then "public service loan forgiveness", and have been denied three times already.) It's also to get back as much of who I was before, with the sad realization that I knew internally I had to become someone new while mourning the loss of myself. Mourning for the loss of someone else is one thing, but mourning the loss of yourself is a very dark emotion that requires an extraordinary amount of shadow work, healing, maintenance, and help.

I remember taking the turn past the church and heading to that corner. I recall hanging by my seat belt over the driving stick in the middle, head down over the passenger seat. The seat belt was so tight that I had a scar across my chest. Just a thin line for the longest time. I was confused, lifting my head, and all I could see was white. I couldn't hear anything at all. It was silent, and everything was white. Every airbag had deployed, and that's why I was seeing white. The silence transitioned, and I began to hear a massive ringing in my head. It was the most deafening sound I have ever heard, and that's a lot coming from a Reading Specialist who has worked with thousands of kids by this time. I was more confused than afraid at the moment because I truly didn't comprehend I had just been struck yet. I heard OnStar come on asking me to respond, and I wasn't saying anything because I was still in the process of the accident. He hit me a second time, slamming my side of the car again, and it came flooding to me that I was in a car alongside a cliff. I was putting it together that I was being struck by a car, and at that moment, all I thought was, "Oh my God, he's going to take my legs out or hit me off this cliff". Yes, I thought "he," and who knows why it was just a thought I had. After the second hit, I, in true fight or flight mode, reached over to the passenger assistance handlebar above the passenger side and grabbed it with my right arm. While escaping, I can still hear OnStar repeating, "Ma'am, we need you to respond…" My left arm already felt like it was on fire. It was welted up and looked like and felt like if I touched my skin, it was going to just peel off. I yanked hard with my right arm and pulled my body weight to the right side using the infamous "oh shit" handlebar to open that door. I stumbled out and went straight for the rock wall and hung onto it for dear life. I was grateful to get out of the car but had no energy to move yet. I could hear a commotion behind me, and I layed on the wall trying to get vision and my wits about me. With my head down, I heard a man yell, "oh my god, there was a passenger" followed by the words, "the driver must be dead! Who yells that? Really when I think of that to this day, I start crying. I felt sick to my stomach with angst, and for obvious reasons, I just couldn't pull myself together. The pain on my left side was unbearable, and speaking clearly was not something I was able to do. I walked to the front of the home on the corner and just started to sit down out of fatigue and shock. A man and his female companion came to me and asked me if there was a driver. I told him that I was the driver.

As I stared forward at the drunk driver and car in shock, I witnessed a woman screaming at the drunk driver to stop through his driver's window as well as another man. I even heard someone yell out, “he’s drunk”. Someone reached in and turned his car off. They took his keys to stop the car. They pulled out a very large clear vodka bottle with a red label on it which I later found out was a Smirnov’s vodka bottle. While I was holding my left arm, witnessing this, the man who was helping me started apologizing to me.

He asked me to sit down, and they gave me water. They called 911 (but my car had already deployed for help because I have OnStar). Side note, since this accident, the only car I have purchased is the GMC Terrain because OnStar saved me by deploying help faster than anyone was even able to call 911. I am currently on my 4th consecutive GMC Terrain since this accident (of course, after I paid it off, I have to give his one to my son and will need to purchase a 5th one soon). I even sent correspondence to GMC explaining this as I would be perfect for a commercial, but they were uninterested. Can't say a lady didn't try, but it's true. I have stayed with these Terrains because I feel safe.

The helpful witness were apologizing to me, telling me that he was tailing the drunk driver attempting to call 911 but wasn't fast enough. Jumping forward recently, in December 2022, I was having an argument with my 15-year-old son in the car while driving home. Nothing in particular, just normal Mom and son banter, and I looked in my rearview mirror. There was minimal space between my bumper and the car behind me. I literally yelled, "shut up right now we have a problem," and floored the gas pedal. This road is almost unpredictable with the extreme amount of dangerous curves in the road. High speeds are not welcomed and posted by law. I had no choice. I did my best to keep my eye on the turns as well as how fast this car approached. He was swerving all over the road. He sped up as I sped up and started driving in the opposite lane completely. I thought, "OMG, he's under the influence somehow. I could, this time, see a younger male driving, and he looked younger than me. My son now starts yelling and grabs the same handlebar that I used to escape my accident in 2014. My trigger was activated, but I remained calm. I had a split second to decide around which turn I was going to veer off the road clearly to let this car pass, hoping he doesn't follow and slam into us.

I drove towards a driveway and, with a sharp turn, slammed on the brakes to the side, driving across the lawn while the person kept going. My son was traumatized, and I was doing everything I could to not fall apart and start crying. Unsuccessfully I explained that my PTSD was activated, and this is exactly what must have happened with the witness in 2014. My son wanted me to call 911, but I was stuck in a PTSD reaction mixed with guilt. It made me reminisce about the man apologizing to me for not being fast enough to call 911. The roads were dangerous. My son yelled out, "speed up and go get him so we can call it in". It was a teaching moment. I spoke about my accident, and my PTSD, he saw me crying, and I explained that I would forever have a fear when he drives. I'm experienced, and had I not been so aware and such a defensive driver, we would have been smashed from behind aggressively. I already wrote about this accident and have to come back and insert this new PTSD experience because I now fully understand why this man was apologizing to me for not being fast enough to call 911. I had no judgment then and still have no judgment. I was in a compromising situation, and so was he back then. This kind witness, who was apologizing, went on to tell me that he saw this visibly drunk driver enter his car. He was attempting to call the driver in and request help, but he was already moving up the hill as he watched him crash into me. His guilt was bothering him, and he was visibly shaken as I had just shared, knowing firsthand the experience of what he was feeling.

The ambulance showed up and put me on the stretcher, which was incredibly painful. I did not want to be on my back due to the pain being unbearable. I kept asking to please let me sit up because I was in so much pain. For safety reasons and not knowing the extent of my injuries, they kept me lying down. Anger flooded through me as I realized I had been struck by a drunk driver. True story, allow me to digress, my ex-husband was struck by a drunk driver in May 2006, and the driver did a hit and run but was found. Then I was hit in June 2014, and he, too, tried to flee the scene of the accident unsuccessfully.

The ambulance ride was not moving yet, and I was getting agitated. I just wanted to get to the hospital and off of the stretcher. It was then that the EMT told me they were going to remove me from the ambulance and take the other driver to the hospital first. I went wild with anger because I knew the other driver was drunk. I also knew that it would be a period of time before a second ambulance would come to collect me, especially given the position of the accident and the traffic that was backed up on both sides. They decided to proceed to take me to the hospital, which was the most uncomfortable ride in my life, physically and emotionally.

We finally began heading to the hospital, and I was in so much pain. I remember the ride with vivid detail because the EMT was arguing with me that "I don't know the details of the other driver, and he wasn't drunk." He went on to give me a lecture about not assuming and was being oddly defensive about the scenario, which was really making me angry. I found out later that the drunk driver was a retired NY Police Detective who had a previous alcohol addiction. The accident is public record, and I'm not out to destroy anyone. He made that decision, and this is what happened. He will have to carry the consequences of that forever. Yet while in pain and emotionally upset that this EMT was being rude and arguing with me. I didn't understand, but it was later revealed to me through my lawyer. Of course, I can only say my side of the story, but I remember him not being friendly at all. I've had emergency help for a good portion of my life for various reasons before this accident. I already had experience with EMT's, and this was not my usual experience. He was defensive, and there's no other way to describe his words and actions.

When I arrived in the emergency room, everyone swarmed around me quickly, asking me many questions and trying to evaluate me. I wanted to get off my back and kept asking to do so, but I was not allowed to move. They started to remove my clothing, and one nurse yelled out, "wait, I can save that shirt, it's cute. I can get it off of her without ripping it". She managed to get everything off carefully. I was wearing a mossy green lace tank top, a long thin tan silky skirt, and gold glitter sneakers. Anyone who knows me knows that I love wearing sparkly things. Not for the attention, it's just because I like it, just the same as preferring the colors blue and red. The lights were blinding, and I could barely keep my eyes open to them. My head had an unbearable sharp pain, and the right side of my head, above my right ear following it to the top, felt bruised. The vision in my right eye was blurry, and my eye was constantly watering. My parents weren't able to get down to me because they were not healthy enough to drive themselves to the hospital, which was 1 hour and 20 minutes away from them. I was alone for a period of time because my ex-husband worked 1 hour away, and his father was taking care of my son, who was at the baseball field that I didn't return to. It's not the first time I was alone in a hospital for serious health reasons fighting off pain and fear.

Oddly enough, this man came to bring me to get x-rays done, and as he was pushing me through the doors, someone called out to him, "not her, the man needs x-rays first". I yelled out, "You mean the drunk driver that hit me?" The transfer person looked at me and said, "That's the man that drove into you"? I said, "Yes," and he continued to take me to get my x-rays done. I've had plenty of x-rays done growing up over the years for various reasons, but this was the most difficult set of x-rays I ever needed to sit still for. My neck, back, and head were in an amount of pain I had never experienced. I was sure there were broken bones from the radiating pain I was feeling in all directions. They also completed a CT scan of my head. They put me back into the ER room that I arrived in, and the police officer came in to speak to me. By then, my ex-in-laws had arrived and had gone to my vehicle and collected things as well as took pictures. My ex-mother-in-law and I had a lot of similar qualities, always making sure we kept detailed information in life, generally speaking. Ironically my car was towed by a company that states on the business card, "Used police cars-towing service." By then, my ex-husband had also arrived.

The officer told us that the driver was refusing to take a breathalyzer, but they were able to take his blood to see exactly how drunk he was. It wasn't until later on that I discovered from my lawyer that he was .436. Yes, I typed those numbers correctly. He was a tall man with a decent size. I was still baffled by how a person could be alive after drinking to that extent. No fractures were seen on the x-rays despite my horrendous pain. They literally gave me

Ibuprofen and sent me out the door. I was scared and baffled because this level of pain was not normal, and I knew something was terribly wrong.

I remember arriving home and sitting in the dining room chair, stunned, not knowing what to do. I was happy to see my son and even more grateful that he missed this accident. It was only a matter of about 7-10 minutes that he missed being in this accident with me. It could have been fatal for him. My friend did stop by and give me flowers from my colleagues and a gift certificate to Diamond Mills which was my favorite place. Seemingly to her, and to them through her, I was okay. As a matter of fact, she said to me, "You're lucky, people have had way worse". It's true, but at the time, she had no idea of what was about to unfold in regard to injuries received from this car crash. I, on the other hand, knew something was very wrong.

A background piece of information that is important about how I "fared" during this accident is that I had been in top physical condition at 37 years old during this accident. Six months prior, I had been training in Tang Soo Do with my son (a form of Karate). I was at the weight that I was when I was 25 years old. Ironically I started this training six months prior because I had a High School student threaten to shoot me pretending to have a gun in his pocket during class. I will not get into the specifics of this for legal reasons, but it was the initial push to be able to defend myself if I ever had to in general. Matched with the consistent threat of school shootings, I decided to train and protect not only myself but any child who was under my supervision. It was a scary wake-up call that ended up saving my life. I was also going to the gym religiously at the time and using the Elliptical. I was not a runner at the time, but my son and I were always extremely athletic and active together, rollerblading while he biked, jumping on bounce houses in different places, etc. It's very strange that the timing of this lined up the way it did. I am grateful that I listened to my inner guidance.

Before this accident, in January 2014, I had an MRI of the brain because I had been experiencing some odd illness that had been floating around the building (no surprise now since COVID rocked the world), but I was concerned about a virus or lyme that was making me have strange headaches. I was told nothing was wrong with my brain previously, and it went undiagnosed. I had thoughts about Lyme at the time, but there was also a virus going around the building. In the past, this was dismissed, and now, after COVID, we understand how viruses can be debilitating. This means I had a comparison MRI of the brain from January 2014 to one done on me after the accident on June 16, 2014.

By fate alone, there was a comparison MRI of what they could see before and after the accident. Just typing that date made me freeze in my tracks. My father hit his head with a fatal blow on June 14, 2020, and my Mother passed away on this exact date of June 16, 2020, so typing this documented date made my heart stop just now. This has triggered me, and I just had a flashback and gasped for air. I am breathing to remain calm.

After being sent home from the hospital, it was scheduled for me to have an MRI of the Right shoulder, with a bone scan after the accident. I went in for an MRI of my spine, the left spine as they wrote it, and the left hip on June 13, 2014. That was quite a few days after the collision. I recall feeling angered and shocked they were waiting so long to see what could be wrong with me since I was feeling so much pain.

I was terrified to get the MRI's done because I could not lay on my back. I could if I was on my bed, but not on a flat hard surface because the pain was intolerable even with medication. I remember having earplugs in, covering my eyes, and doing my best to lay perfectly still while thriving in pain with that sequence of what sounds like a jackhammer in different patterns. It seemed like forever in there, and I did everything I could not to cry because I didn't want to have to do the MRIs again. As it was, I already had to do three of them. At home, I literally laid in bed in agony on several medications at once to try and dull the pain. My son, who was seven years old, would come in and want to cuddle with me like we always did, and I would have to tell him that he couldn't touch me because I was in so much pain. He was heartbroken watching me be a completely different person. He brought home his school folder, and I opened it up, and there was a drawing inside. It was a woman lying in bed and a small boy next to the bed. The sentence said, "My Mom got hurt and stays in bed". Just writing that sentence has me tearing up as I attempt to keep telling you my story. The searing pain in my left index finger kept me awake all night despite the heavy painkillers. It didn't show in an MRI, but the chiropractor had to readjust my finger, and the nerve pain stopped. However, I was unable to use that finger at all. I had to go to physical therapy, and when that was over, I still wasn't healed and had to go to a second hand specialist. I described this entire process with my Mom, of course. She had rheumatoid arthritis and needed hand therapy later as well. I was able to show her the way and make her feel more comfortable about the experience. With all of my therapies, doctor visits, etc., I was right there explaining all of this to my Mom. She was my biggest cheerleader. Every time I wanted to quit, she never let me give up. She called me her bulldog. I had a long journey to go, and little did I know at the time that all of these therapies I was doing to get my life back, she was about to do as well. She never had any fear because she knew that not only did I know where to go for help, but exactly what to do to try and save her. I will say she was a lot more stubborn than I was about carrying out the PT sessions.

I was sent to a neurosurgeon to review the results of the MRI of the brain, and he told me that the good news was that my brain was not bleeding. I questioned how I could sense odd things happening to me, such as blurred vision in the right eye, the right eye watering all day and night without ceasing, sensitivity to sunlight and sounds, forgetting words, and not being able to stand up straight. I would be standing and just topple over to the side like someone pushed me. Multitasking was, before the accident, my talent, but now keeping my focus on one sentence seemed too far-fetched. I would be holding a glass, and it would just drop out of my hand. I started to lose my handwriting. It started to become dangerous for me to carry anything that I thought would break if it was dropped. The Neurosurgeon told me that the best thing I could do for this head trauma was to "go back to normal" and try to do everything that I could before. I was training for Karate before the accident and attempted to return, but I couldn't balance just standing up. I couldn't count and move at the same time. I couldn't recall patterns and formations that I had done repetitively, and taking new directions was impossible. I knew something was wrong. However, I watched myself decline and was yelling in every direction for help, but because it was an invisible illness, it was being pushed to the side.

My first lawyer was the person, along with the main doctor who was taking care of me during this accident, who advised me to keep a journal of everything happening to me on a day-to-day basis. I was unable to return to teaching for the remainder of June 2014. I also was unable to return to teaching as of September 2014. I was so anxious about returning to work I attempted to return in October 2014, and I was called to the office and was respectfully asked to go home and take the time to heal. They did it with the best of intentions, but I was devastated. I was not a danger to my third Grade students at the time and could teach, but it was very noticeable that I was in pain and trying hard. I had a neck brace on, my left hand taped because of my pointer finger that I couldn't use, my neck and right shoulder had the kinesthetic tape, and my left hip had the tape as well. The only bandage missing was one around my head to let everyone know that I was working with a brain injury.

Returning back to June after being sent home right away from the emergency room, I had never experienced muscle spasms before other than a quick foot or leg cramp, menstrual cycles, miscarriage, or child labor. I've even had three surgeries for Endometriosis (one of them lasting 3.5 hours when I was 19). I knew what pain was, but this surpassed it. This was over my entire body and felt like muscles so tight it wanted to pull apart. It's still difficult to put into words, but if you have experienced this level of pain, then you are probably nodding your head in agreement with my attempted description of this pain. It was the first time I was ever introduced to muscle relaxers. My doctor at the time was surprised that I was sent home with only an Ibuprofen. He immediately called in muscle relaxers explaining the trauma that was done to my body from the impact of all of the airbags being deployed at the same time apart from the crash. The side effects of the muscle relaxers, Percocet, Xanax, Naproxen while the deficit was growing in abilities to my head injury, were quickly demonstrating a need for evaluation. We needed to revisit the injury and treatments taken. I was sent to the neuropsychologist for an evaluation, and it was a feeling that I couldn't describe. Ecstatic, I was to hear there was an actual reason for the difficulties I was having, but realizing it was a brain injury and possibly permanent damage was devastating simultaneously.

Chapter 2

After a few months, in the month of October, I had enough evidence that an evaluation for a brain injury was needed. I kept a journal that I wrote in every day to log whatever pain I was having at that time. Was the pain the same, or had it changed? Did I notice any patterns of why it was changing? What medicines did I take that was effective or ineffective? I journaled my emotions as each day passed. I even wrote down things that happened that I could do before but was unable to do with this injury developing deeper. While journaling, I noticed that I started losing my handwriting and speech. It is my line of works to understand how the functions of actual handwriting work, including holding of the writing utensil and use of fine motor coordination. When I put the pen in my right hand, it suddenly felt like I was left-handed. Meaning the pen felt completely foreign, and I knew to "pinch the pen" and did so, forcing myself to take what I knew to do in my profession. When I started to write, it was slow to make it from my mind to the paper. I used to have incredibly neat handwriting, and it was nothing of the sort. It was a major red flag that something was terribly wrong. Still, to this day, in the year 2023, if I try to write too quickly, I will begin misspelling words because something happens when I rush myself. It's not just spelling the words either. I literally, after writing the first five words, start losing the ability to form the actual letters and have to slow down to write. It's not speed. It's the actual formation of the letters. I see it right away and catch it with diligence, so to everyone else, it's unnoticeable. I'm just super aware of it and concentrate on making sure everything gets written the way it needs to. I do not have this issue when typing. How does that work? Why am I able to type freely, typing literally approximately 64 words per minute? If I have to focus on creating the letters, it takes attention away from the process of the words? Who would be able to describe this better than a Reading Specialist who works with students who have special needs?

I called my first lawyer nervously after the start of these scary symptoms. He was not surprised it was going to take a few months to "show itself," meaning the symptoms of a brain injury. Sometimes it takes a few months to truly see the impact. I knew I had something seriously wrong because two days after the accident, my right eye was weeping. I mean continuously weeping all day, all night, never ceasing. I had a rash under my right eye from the constant tears dripping. It was like my body was crying without me being involved in the actual process. The top right part of my head felt bruised, and my right eye vision blurred. I noticed that I didn't remember dreams any more. This broke my heart. I was terrified that my spiritual gift was also gone. I've always had incredibly vivid dreams that often contained messages.

I've even had visions of things to come (premonitions) and was able to relay information to people. My dreams completely stopped. This cut off the gateway I had to reach my spiritual side. I was also plagued by the inability to sleep for days. I could no longer remember information, and I had to use millions of post-it notes, notebooks, and pieces of paper strewn everywhere to keep my life moving forward. It was the recommendation of my neuropsychologist and psychologist to use my cell phone to keep notes as well, which worked out much better. My phone had become my electronic lifeline, my brain. I used to have a photographic memory. I would listen to lectures and be able to recall every detail months later. All of this was gone immediately after the car crash. The falling over, dropping things, slurred speech, inability to recall words, or even understand what someone was saying to me took months to show up. I caught it quickly because of what I do for a living. I'm a Reading Specialist who, at that point, taught for 11-12 years working with Special needs students. I used everything I taught them to compensate and survive. I basically went into "work mode" myself and did whatever I needed to do to get my life back.

When I returned to work after being deemed mentally disabled for over a year, I obviously had to fight to get a routine back while having a brain injury and PTSD. It would only “show itself” occasionally, and I’ll do my best to give you a few examples. I made sure that I shared my story briefly with my students so they were aware and understood. A rare example would be something like this, where I would go to say a word, and the word would come out completely different. For example, and this really happened; I was walking down the hall and saw someone who had fallen earlier. I yelled out, “Ohhh honey, I’m glad you're okay you're such a tramp”. I laughed because I had two options, cry out of embarrassment or laugh. People know exactly what happened to me. I yelled, “CHAMP, CHAMP, you’re such a CHAMP. I’m so proud of you”. It’s very rare now when this happened during the first part of this brain injury in 2014, it was just an every-hour occurrence. Quite often, when I’m worn down from an impending illness or just fatigued for whatever reason, I will be able to see the word in my head, like having a vision for those who are spiritually gifted. I will focus on the first letter and be stuck on it, not able to pull the word from my mind out to verbalize it. It’s not often now, but during the first three years, this was a consistent issue. I would cry out of frustration because I couldn’t get the words that I knew out to communicate properly. That’s why I know my career saved me. I have already worked with Special Needs students and have seen this frustrating response in young children to age 18. Right before my car accident, I was given a student to work with who was very young and was in a car accident and suffered a head injury as well. I still remember everything about this beautiful student to this day. I truly was blessed working with her, as it was right before my accident. I also have a Down syndrome nephew who I have loved and adored since the minute I ever laid eyes on him. We have a special bond. My family members, at this time, already knew how to be caretakers and help each other, guiding me toward rehabilitation. Quite often, when I would get tired and want to "give up," one of them was always there to swat me on the rear end and tell me to get going like the wild black beauty horse that my Psychologist referred me as.

I also lost peripheral vision. The view I had was smaller. I could not see all the way to the right or left. This was not a good feeling for me as I was already hyper-vigilant due to PTSD. I even had trouble reading any of my work on the computer screens. I had to print everything out in order to be able to read, reread, and write on it to attempt to store it in short-term memory in hopes it would eventually make it to long-term memory storage. I would see words in my mind that were not on the page. Vice versa, I would omit words (completely not seeing them), and they were right there in print. For example, after I returned to work to teach (I was out for 1.5 years, 2 years with the summers included) I was teaching my favorite group of second-grade students ever. I told them about my accident, and they were so happy to help whenever things got tough for me. It was genuine love and adoration mutually. I would write a sentence on the board and step back and read it out loud to them. They would giggle and say, Mrs. Kane (I wasn't divorced at that time), it's missing a word. I would say, "No, I see it". I would give them the dry-erase marker, and they loved fixing it. I learned to sometimes play with them and do it on purpose, but they were definitely there to assist. They never made me feel inadequate, and it was a shared, vulnerable, loving respect. You can tell it was one of my favorite groups ever. All of them not only got back on the reading level but exceeded expectations. We as a group were so motivated as a unit to be one to become the best version of ourselves. Jumping forward, one of my students from this group was also in a major accident, and it devastated me to hear of this. I was lucky to have been moved to a higher grade level to teach (even though my true talent is working with young energies) at the time and was closely located. I did everything I could do in my power to help him physically and emotionally inside the building, having many conversations with his Mother and future teachers explaining how this injury demonstrated itself. PTSD also plays a huge role in someone's ability to rehabilitate.

Speaking of the urge to step into the light publicly to share my experiences, I recently made a video for sharing. It was about music one day from the past while I had a brain injury. A talented musician came to work in our school system when I returned to work. He was an Interim principal for us. I stopped him in the hall one time and said, "You have a doctorate in music, right". He answered yes and asked me, "why"? I said, "I need to ask you a serious question, and you will only be able to guess the answer, but I'm curious about your point of view on this". He smiled. I told him that unannounced sounds were unbearable. Lights hurt my eyes, and I even had to narrow the length of time being spent in direct sunlight because I would get headaches. I've even had lightbulbs removed from the ceilings to make the lights seem less like they are trying to land a jet in my classroom. Being in the hallways, even trying to approach the cafeteria or auditorium when it was full, was excruciating to me. However, when I'm in my car and I am listening to music, I am able to listen to it quite loudly when no pain or difficulties would arise from doing so. He said, "Wow. That's very interesting, and I don't really know what the answer is to that because I don't know about brain injuries". I shared that in my line of work, which borders Reading/Speech/Special Education/ School Psychologist/ Social worker/Counselor (every Reading Specialist on this planet is nodding their heads in agreement right now), sounds are extremely important and are and have been my gift. I speak Spanish (although I definitely need to refresh some higher-level vocabulary), and I didn't lose any of it. I didn't lose any of the Greek and Latin word root knowledge. I didn't lose anything in regard to teaching or knowing what to do in my "specialty area". I was even a voice major in college, first heading for performance arts or Music teacher, switched to Spanish teacher, taking Spanish and French. Then became an Early Education Teacher with a Concentration in Spanish. Everything I work with involves sounds and speaking. I also spoke to my neuropsychologist and psychologist about this.

My Neuropsychologist Victor Zelek, Ph.D., and Psychologist Mark Hammel, Ph.D., due to their overlapping professions within the same vicinity while being near the same age bracket, were aware of each other. They both found me fascinating and entertaining because not only did I have a brain injury and PTSD, I was an intelligent Reading Specialist. I make jokes all the time, "well, I was smart," and when people hear me say that, they get so upset and hug me. My colleagues, friends, and family tell me they are so proud of me and everything I have gone through. My Psychologists and I were constantly having discussions about what ailment belonged to which category. "Was that the brain injury or the PTSD"? Dr. Zelek would explain that it's the "brain injury," and my psychologist Dr. Hammel would explain it's "PTSD". In reality, they both overlap and mimic each other. They were aware of this as well. Only through therapy sessions would we be able to have a discussion and make educational guesses as to why it was one or the other. The analogy is the same for both. My brain had limited battery life. When the battery would start to get low, some odd things would start to happen. My words would slur. My vision would blur. I'd start to get emotional or upset. I learned to recognize this and how to handle it to "recharge". The problem with this is that with a brain injury and PTSD, the battery was already draining. By the time you recognize the "low battery" signal, you do not have much time to rescue yourself. That was during the first 4-5 years of rehabilitation. Now that these side effects have lessened drastically, almost to a non-existent point, it is easy for me to identify a time to take a break. I've had countless conversations with Dr. Hammel and Dr. Zelek about taking a break when I see the signs. I was still trying to be the highly charged self-sufficient "Keli" I was before that simply just couldn't exist in this newer version. My sharing of experiences is to demonstrate how incredibly difficult it is to maneuver these while trying to rehabilitate and create a new self. Discovering who we are as humans is an incredibly spiritual and time-consuming task without stripping yourself of the ability to think, speak, express yourself, or even be able to stand in your own skin from the effects of PTSD.

The brain injury hit me in a very specific area of my brain. It is, without a doubt, the right side of my head, meaning over my right eye. The side effects of all of the rehabilitations I chose have greatly diminished and only appear when I am completely stressed, carrying too many responsibilities, or I am simply coming down with something. Keep in mind I teach in an elementary building that contains around 800-900 students and then add teaching staff and very much-needed building staff. When I first started therapy, both Dr. Zelek and Dr. Hammel would have to remind me that having this injury is an invisible illness. If I walked around with a bandage on my head, then it would be a visual cue or reminder for others to have more patience with me. People would see that I was walking around and attempting to return to normal and would forget that I was still in healing mode. I would often have to say, "please repeat that " with people getting visually upset because they were thinking, "oh my God, how many times do I need to repeat this to her". I used to cry so hard about this because I was doing the best that I could do what the first Neurologist said which was to "try to get back to your normal routine as much as possible". That was not the advice of my Neuropsychologist and Psychologist. I would have to say everywhere I go, "I was in an accident, and I'm going to need a little extra help," before I did anything. I learned that if I was direct and upfront about it, there was no room for error or attitude from anyone else. It simply was extra energy that I didn't have to expend because all of my energy was being used to heal myself. My family and friends would get upset, stating that "I don't have to tell everyone I see about my accident". It was my own compensating device, and it allowed me to not second guess what anyone was saying, doing, or thinking. It was my Reading Specialist inside me who was thinking, "Let's just get straight to the point because I don't have spare time and need to figure this out". Always keeping that "bandage on my head" visual that everyone else couldn't see, I just figured I'll announce it then because they just can't see it. Very much like my spiritual work when I have visions or hear messages that they don't see. Sometimes, depending if the person is open or not, I will share the information.

In the beginning, I would cry and struggle when I couldn't keep time or reverse numbers. This injury remains in a very tiny and very specific domain in my brain. It is based solely on anything to do with numbers repeating them in verbal or written form. I have a giant stadium clock in my classroom because looking at an analog clock gives me some weirdness, and I still don't know how to refer to this OCD effect where I can't just look at the clock and memorize the time. An example of this is I know very well what 3:15, 3:30, and 3:45, etc., all look like. However, I can't stop myself from counting by fives from 12 over to get to the time. If you give me a test, I'll give you the right time. I can teach it, I just can't stop myself from making that repetitive motion. I did not do this before my brain injury. It was slowing me down, and I had difficulty at work because of this. I have to pick classes up and drop them back off while completing the teaching tasks I have planned. My school Psychologist stated that she would get me a stadium clock. Everyone who passes my door knows exactly why that clock is there and loves it. The kids love it because I will announce times, and they help keep the class moving or remind me when time is running out. We collectively work as a unit mastering the art of time management. However, it was in its glory days when I was haunted by this with all the other problems a brain injury presents. I was having trouble even while using my cell phone as my virtual brain, so to speak. Constantly showing up at the wrong doctor's office.

You have already read that I saw a Neurologist, Neuropsychologist, and Psychologist and even had a School Psychologist that I would meet with from time to time at work. That's not even close to the rest of the people that I went to in order to heal with the level of rehabilitation that I have completed. I was constantly showing up at one place when I was supposed to be at another office. Meanwhile, I was driving incredibly long distances in order to get these rehabilitation visits completed. I drive 2 hours a day, teaching and an hour south of where I live. I would drive back to my home area and cross the Rhinebeck Bridge and drive another 15 minutes for my Neurofeedback appointments. Dr. Zelek would write messages for the week, guidance really or a focus point, on a post-it note. I kept them, of course. He wrote in one particular piece, "Share a monthly schedule with husband. Print a hard copy of the schedule and on the phone as well as a backup schedule". My doctor started sending me messages and texts or calls to remind me which one I was rushing to while trying to work. DR. Zelek also drew me a graph one time explaining the fatigue I experienced and how much energy I lost having PTSD and a brain injury. Dr. Zelek drew two arrows moving in opposite diagonal lines, only crossing in the middle (looks like an x). The red arrow facing down was "stress, aggravation, and frustration. The blue arrow rising was clear thinking and problem-solving. Dr. Zelek explained that this simply means that the more stressed, angry, frustrated, or upset you are, the less you are capable of clear thinking and making good decisions. Another note Dr. Zelek gave me stated, "Stress is not what happens to me. Stress is how I react to what happens to me". How many inspirational posts have we all seen using this phrase in our lifetime? I was doing my best to make sure that I remained "level" because the more "level" I could be, the better I could function. My goal was to blend in and function and get my life back. My years of working with special needs individuals helped me blend with the compensating devices that I have been instructing others to use my entire career. At that point, I truly practiced what I preached in order to be productive.

Dr. Zelek and Dr. Hammel did their best to keep me from returning to work as long as they could because of the healing needed and the massive responsibilities I would be walking back into. I remember crying so hard at Dr. Zelek's office many times, sobbing that "I want my life back". Typing that just now brought tears to my eyes because it was the most painful emotion and place I have ever been. I watched myself disappear and was emotionally and quite literally fighting for my life. Keep in mind that while you are reading all of this that I was going through, I had a 7-year-old son whose heart was breaking witnessing this struggle to rehabilitate with his childhood at times being stolen from him. In the same way that I lost time with my dying parents, he lost time in his childhood with me being ill as well.

The evaluation for a neuropsychologist consisted of a few things. Every visit you have with a neuropsychologist before beginning Neurofeedback, they evaluate your emotional state and any difficulties that may have occurred recently before conducting the test or working with you. It's the first part of every session. They need this information to compare how you're actually performing, much like what I do for a living as a Reading Specialist. In my profession, I'll quickly speak with students to pick up mannerisms, motivation levels, or an emotion that may have come up that day due to a certain circumstance. Observation is part of the process as much as the actual "scoring". I understood this process and complied above and beyond to the best of my ability each time because the only goal I had was to succeed. My goal was to show exactly what was happening and follow directions explicitly so I could heal.

One of the major issues I had at hand was that I was deemed "mentally disabled," but it was an invisible illness. I still looked the same, and people would speak to me in a fast-paced speech ridden with idioms and sarcasm at times. I was not able to interpret this. I have a naturally playful and strong sense of humor. I was witty and able to give it back as fast as it came in the past. I found myself struggling to receive simple directions with more than one step at a time. I felt numb like I was unable to laugh or emote what I wanted to others, feeling inadequate because I knew that I "used to be smart". The brain injury didn't just affect my speech, actions, and abilities. It also changed how I was feeling and many of the dynamics that I had with people, so much so that I had to cut them out completely. Their lives went on, and no words were sent in any form of communication. It was just silent. It caused a lot of emotional pain and frustration because these people were my "friends" whom I would speak to multiple times a day which just dropped to an eerie silence. DR. Hammel later explained to me that this is not because people don't care, they just don't know what to say or do. I now understand this, and after years of therapy, I am okay. There are only a few people that I cared about to share my story and point of view and heal the connection. Explaining myself or feeling bad about them moving forward while I was stuck in a world of silence wasn't helping any of us. I changed my cell phone number, blocked people on Social Media, and moved on, trying to create an old/new Keli to survive. I didn't have extra energy or time to continue wallowing in the sadness that came with this accident or how other people seemed concerned in the beginning and just faded into the background. After eight years of therapy, I understand what was happening, but at the time, you aren't thinking anything but the feeling of frustration, anger, and sadness while trying to survive. That "pre-accident Keli" I referred to while leaving that baseball field wasn't, isn't here anymore. I have room for errors now. I feel free of judgment. I am no longer concerned if someone needs to go their separate ways anymore. I am not stressing about being perfect because that simply does not exist. It certainly can't exist with what happened to me now, either. I am 100% okay with this now.

One of the first sessions completed with my neuropsychologist was a meeting with my ex-husband (husband at the time) about the use of sarcasm. It was a major part of our relationship to make jokes and take jabs at each other wittingly. When I was no longer able to process regular sentences, obviously, it would be unattainable for me to interpret his use of sarcasm. The doctor brought us into his office and sat us down on the couch together. He explained my brain injury in detail to my ex-husband. He discussed the severity of my injury and wanted to talk about the different paths I now have to take in conversations. He asked my ex-husband what his favorite part of our relationship was. His response was, "we joke around and use sarcasm". The doctor explained that my ability to understand and use sarcasm was no longer an option. I would not be able to process the jokes, and it will significantly change the relationship. The doctor wanted my ex-husband to know and used these exact words; "Keli has been permanently injured, and the use of sarcasm is just not going to be something that she can use or understand anymore. If you want to have a marriage with her, you will have to change as she has changed. You both will have to learn a new way of being together". I cried hearing this. It was a pivotal point in my life, and I often can still see myself sitting on that couch. From that point forward, things were never the same in our marriage ever again.

There was another very emotional incident that happened in regard to my wedding ring at this time. Due to the constant resizing of the ring that I had, the diamonds were shifted. They told me that they couldn't keep the ring insured if I took it back because the diamonds couldn't be secured and that one of the stones could fall out. Since they deemed it "not safe," I had to pick out a different ring. Mind you, I am in a mentally disabled state with PTSD and have already suffered severe losses at this point. I went "wild black beauty" as Dr. Hammel lovingly called me once. I had already experienced so much loss at this point. I was thinking to God, is this a joke? I want to share with you a true story about wedding rings between my ex-husband and me. On the honeymoon, his wedding band was titanium, and while swimming in the ocean in Cozumel, Mexico, it slipped off his finger, and we found it. We returned home to get it resized and were told that it was impossible to resize titanium and had to get a new one. We always made jokes, "well, that's not even your real wedding band". On our first anniversary, I had a close friend who ran a jewelry store, and we "upgraded" my ring. I didn't even feel really bad about it because neither one of us had our "real ring". It was important at the time, but it sure isn't now. When this woman said to me about having to pick out a new ring, part of me was like, "oh my God, what is with us and these rings"? I cried hysterically to Dr. Zelek and Dr. Hammel. Dr. Zelek asked to have my ex-husband pick out a new wedding ring for me. I went in a few times and was so overwhelmed I left with nothing solved, and now I was more upset that I wasn't wearing the ring as opposed to picking one. We returned to the store, and he picked out a new ring. Often I joked that it was a sign of us not supposed to be married while fighting. Well, the joke is on me, I guess, because now we're divorced, and I don't wear either of the rings. I did wear them off and on for a brief period of time. I'm certainly traumatized and don't want to go back in and pick a ring to wear. I miss wearing rings like that terribly, but I absolutely have PTSD trauma response and would not be able to go in and pick a ring. Whoever the next love of my life is, hopefully, will understand this and just know me better than I know myself and be able to accomplish that task by himself someday if it ever arises. Jumping ahead when I was waiting in the COVID vaccination line, while newly separated, I wasn't wearing my rings, and I kept hiding my hand. I felt embarrassed to be single. I guess more so that my marriage didn't work, but who would know that out of the hundreds of people, I was standing in line with? I just needed someone to know me and what I needed. I'm trying to share the traumatic side of emotional events that carried on as I was healing. As you keep reading, you'll start to see how many therapies I went to and see the whole picture. This is just a snapshot of things that happened emotionally that left scars while in the healing process.

Chapter 3

It was very difficult to take these evaluations with the neuropsychologist. He had to continuously stop and settle me because I would get so frustrated. I knew what I was able to do, and what I was demonstrating was scaring me. He was helping me to stop crying anytime I saw my injury “appear”. It’s taken me almost nine years, but now if anything, “blips” is what I call them, and it’s now very rare due to my rehabilitation and efforts, I am able to giggle about it. I allow the people close to me to even giggle with me about it. People have often said these exact words, “Kane, I love how honest and upfront you are about what happened. You have such a great attitude about it. I’m proud of you”.

Confidentiality was not an issue for me while I was rehabilitating. With all the lawyers, insurance companies, etc., I felt I literally had no privacy at all. I’ve been thoroughly vetted to even teach children. I’ve been vetted by the government as power of attorney for my parents, who needed state help. I’m no stranger to the government, so I’ve been checked, and checked, and checked, and I’m just the same good human I’ve always been. Imperfect good human. With that said, I also had a unique scenario with the individual who struck me, which ripped privacy away from me. I had nothing to hide, so I shared my doctor's appointment schedule with my employers. I had to keep "mileage reports" to submit to Insurance, and I documented every single therapy I went to, the address, date, and time and turned it into work. Whether they kept it or not is irrelevant to me. Truth teller, I am, so I shared all of my reports and therapies for Neurofeedback with the School Psychologist at my workplace in the elementary building. She helped me get a 504 for my teaching career. In simple terms, a 504 "is a set of accommodations, or changes in the classroom environment, to help a child follow the regular curriculum. It is less formal and involved than an Individualized Education Program (IEP) and does not change the instruction itself. For example, a student who uses a wheelchair but doesn't need academic support would have a 504 plan". These exist for teachers as well. As long as you are able to carry out all functions of the job needed.

I had/have a 504 plan for PTSD and a brain injury. My asthma was also included after advice given to me. I'll never forget the meeting I had with the person in charge of my 504 plan, the School Psychologist. She told me that I should have the room at a constant temperature because of the drugs that would be resting in my system stored in fatty parts of my liver. Big temperature changes could release some medication in an attempt to process it out of my body, releasing the toxin. I'll also never forget the conversation I had with the Interim Director of Special Education. He knew me before the accident and after. I had a meeting with him about what types of training were needed in the district at the time. I found out that he used to work with people who had brain injuries, and we talked about what had happened to me. He smiled and looked at me as I was trying not to weep, sharing what I had lost and feeling insecure. He told me that he was proud of what I was doing. It was like a teacher telling a student they are proud of them. It meant the world at that time, especially since I knew that he was closer to understanding what I was fighting than anyone else in that school district besides the School Psychologist and my old Middle school principal boss. I always knew she was talented and headed for the stars. She advanced to the Assistant Superintendent and brought the training to our building during a faculty meeting, explaining how to teach students the need to store information from short-term memory to long-term memory. Deep down in my heart, I felt like it was to explain to the staff once and for all what had happened to me and what to expect. However, I keep breaking the mold on what to expect because I want to be the best version of myself that I can be. I'm constantly compensating and surviving while loving life and playing because life is short. Time is relevant. It's always about the moment at hand.

Before diving into the therapies that I went to in order to rehabilitate from this brain injury, I would like to explain how grateful I am for my job and employer. I was able to use sick days when I was deemed "mentally disabled," and when that time was out, they had a sick bank for me to use. When I returned, they made sure that I had the 504 in place. It was not always a smooth transition but a work in progress. Without this support, I would not have had the time or resources to go to the therapies that healed me. I am forever grateful. Dr. Zelek and Dr. Hammel often commented on how lucky I was to be able to receive this help in order to heal. They didn't share anyone's private business but explained how the system worked in order to get insurance coverage or worker's compensation. Jumping forward to the year 2023, I am so lucky to have the administrative boss women team leading me in my career. I am making sure to give a specific shout-out to my Principal, who I always just refer to as "Boss", Nicole Ey. What a breath of fresh air. I have taught in all three buildings, grades K-12, and have had many Principals. I loved many of them, but she has the gift. She was just nominated the 2022 New York State Elementary Principal of the year by the School Administrators Association of New York and the National Association of Elementary School Principals. No surprise because she also received the 2017 Assistant Principal & Nat'l AP of the year of New York. She has had my back and knows exactly what I've been through, and has supported me. She just traveled to Guatemala with the Lifetouch Memory Mission to make a classroom out of recycled bottles. It's a comfort to know you can have someone to go to for guidance. I'm also lucky to have Rebecca Maher as my "Reading Team" Boss, who was there sitting with me in my office while I was sobbing about what I was going through at the time. She also showed compassion while observing that no matter what was crippling me emotionally, I never missed a beat with the kiddos. I was even lucky enough to have my Reading Team member Meredith Smith advance to the Assistant Principal during the pandemic, so it was great to have "Reading Specialist" eyes in the Admin team as well as having a sympathetic and very deep understanding as a former team member to my zany personality and struggles I was overcoming. These women work well together, and it just makes it easier to try your best each day. We've even added a new Assistant Principal, Heather Heidelberg, who reminds me much of my younger "boss" self and is extremely supportive and kind but able to handle the heat gracefully. I'm telling you, it's the Dream Team of Admin. I've been in three buildings, K-12, and teaching for 20 years as a Reading Specialist working with the toughest cases most times. I know what I'm saying when I speak this truth. There is no "perfect," but the camaraderie and teamwork/support makes it perfect.

I've already shared that I went to Dr. Zelek to receive Neurofeedback. I went to his sessions for a little over a year, completing 45 sessions. I am not a doctor, so to be clear, I will use a quote explaining specifically what this is and then, in my own terms, tell you what I can recall from these sessions. I have taken this directly from Dr. Zelek's website, explaining what this process is.

"Neurofeedback (also called Neurotherapy or EEG Biofeedback) is a computer-assisted treatment that enables you to alter your own brain waves. When you can see your own brain waves on a computer screen, you can learn to change them in a direction that improves your brain functioning. Thus, the goal of Neurofeedback is self-regulation.

Biofeedback has been used to help people control their physiological responses, such as relaxing their muscles, increasing temperatures in their hands, lowering their heart rate, reducing sweating, promoting heart rate variability, and normalizing breathing, to name a few. Neurofeedback which is a form of Biofeedback employs brain-computer interfaces and virtual reality settings to allow brainwave training. From a behavioral viewpoint, Neurofeedback is a form of operant conditioning. Once you have conditioned your brain to increase or reduce specific brainwaves (Delta, Theta, Alpha,

Beta, and Gamma) or to improve the symmetry and coherence of those brainwaves, you can improve your brain functioning in areas such as attention, alertness, mental acuity, memory, flexibility, associative thinking, creativity, and calmness. Such mental conditioning or "physical therapy" for the brain improves your "mental posture" and rids you of cognitive problems, just as improved physical posture and muscle tone can rid you of back pain."

Also stated by Dr. Zelek, "EEG Biofeedback has been shown to be particularly beneficial in ADD/ADHD, traumatic brain injury, stroke, epilepsy, depression, alcoholism, Chronic Fatigue Syndrome, brain Lyme, sleep disorders, anxiety, pain control, headaches, stress reduction, autoimmune disorders and other conditions in which brain wave properties are either impaired or not at the optimal level. How can one treatment modality address so many different conditions? Because it addresses the source by fine-tuning the central command unit - your brain".

I'd like to expand on that sentence when Dr. Zelek stated, "How can one treatment modality address so many different conditions". I'd like to use those same words with a different point to make to all the people healing as I have been. One modality of healing will not be enough. I'm describing to you the first step in healing a brain injury, and that was

Neurofeedback. I was also having cranial sacral healing sessions and traditional and cranial Osteopathic treatment at this time. I will describe those in detail shortly, but I'd like to return back to the sessions with Dr. Zelek so you can get a patient's point of view on what I can recall of these sessions.

Dr. Zelek has an extremely calming demeanor. He has a very subtle way of delivering advice, even when I would present my "wild black beauty" side out of frustration with my circumstance. The first part of this therapy is talking about your emotional state at that moment. As a Reading Specialist, I relate to this very well. Before evaluating anyone's true reading potential, I, too, would quickly have a conversation and assess things such as mannerisms or comfortability. If there was something I could say or do quickly, I would in order to have my assessment be as valid as possible. I eliminate distractions, make it comfortable, speak in a friendly manner, etc. For example, if someone is fidgety, I would ask what was bothering them to make them comfortable or get an anxiety ball, whatever they need. Dr. Zelek offered this calming effect and had good advice to give about being "present in the moment". This talent of keeping someone calm in a brain injury and PTSD state is a true talent.

The initial evaluation to determine a brain injury is long. Hours-long, as a matter of fact. It has multiple steps involved. It's explained as a neurological exam that evaluates thinking, motor function (movement), sensory function, coordination, eye movement, and reflexes. Imaging tests, such as CT scans and MRI scans, cannot detect all TBIs (Traumatic Brain Injuries). I'm concerned about sharing the exact parts of the test because I do not want to compromise results for anyone else. I will tell you that tasks are switched and brought back at times. Each time I was brutally aware that I was unable to store information in long-term memory, and it was difficult not to have a traumatic reaction each time. This only complicates things as you need to be in your calmest emotional state in order to perform at your fullest potential. I was literally having flashbacks of nervous students sitting in front of me relating to that exact feeling. It's been close to 9 years now, and I am still extremely sensitive to students' feelings while testing and working with them. Of course, no person is perfect, so I certainly don't claim that in any way, shape, or form. I am claiming that I truly try my best at all times because this has been a major part of my life experience. Matched with the fact that I am a gifted Empath makes me an extra aware person when it comes to human emotions.

The tests on the computer frustrated me when testing my "response time" and motor coordination. For the life of me, whatever I saw would not match up to my response times with my hand. I'm being vague on purpose again, not wanting to compromise any portion of the testing that may be used. I'm very comfortable talking about the actual Neurofeedback training, though. I spoke about this on one of my podcasts with the "movies" that we would watch for training. It was indeed the strangest thing I have ever gone through and one of the most frustrating things. To this day, any time live streaming freezes, I immediately think of my Neurofeedback.

I picked a few movies to watch for the Neurofeedback sessions. Dr. Zelek was kind enough to take the time to look back and share which movies I watched. They were" Young Frankenstein with Gene Wilder, Secondhand Lions, Australia, Baraka, Austin Powers, Azur & Asmar (animation), The Campaign, and Life of Pi. He also shared with me that "the movies only served as the means of giving you instant feedback when your brainwaves misbehaved, meaning it went out of the normal range". I would have wires (sensors) attached with sticky glue to the top of my head on each side that would send data to the computer. I would be sitting comfortably facing the screen playing this movie. If at any time my brain was not in the correct state (within normal range), the movie would stop playing. I'd literally be sitting there completely still, and it would freeze, or stop, and come back on. Initially, it was pretty wild, almost to the point of getting dizzy because it would stop and start so many times. My job was to remain calm, and the movie would recognize this state and start playing. I would get upset sometimes because I truly, in my heart, felt like I was sitting there calmly but was not. If the brain waves were moving too fast or too slow, the movie would stop. As soon as you balance or "normalize," the movie will continue. I would spend multiple visits trying to complete a movie. I also had to play these games that provided immediate feedback. I would get to pick the game, and it's pretty tough for me to recall the details of these games. Again I don't like to talk about too many details because I do not want to comprise test results for anyone else. Professionally speaking, I'm very respectful of this.

Evaluation time was never a fun experience for me. Even after the first evaluation, where I would be able to eliminate the anxiety of what the test actually was and how it felt to take it, I was still just as traumatized each time I was not able to complete a task like I knew I would have been able to do in the past. I even had to be evaluated by the Neuropsychologist from the insurance company to prove that I indeed still needed treatment. The system is set up to watch you like a hawk, so they know exactly when to stop helping you cover the cost of treatments. I remember waiting in Dr. Zelek's office, going into another room for this evaluation not once but a few times. I saw this book sitting there on the coffee table that hadn't been there previously. It was a book by Shel Silverstein titled *The Missing Piece Meets The Big O*. This book is about a missing piece in search of its perfect match. This was clearly about making changes and having experiences to realize how wonderful you are. It also demonstrates that one can adapt and become the missing piece needed independently within yourself. I can't help but feel completely different as I write about it now. At this point in my life, not in the past, I feel like this pertains to my love life. I've gone through so many experiences trying to find my perfect soulmate match. Working with both the past and my current reality, this book fits perfectly fine. That's the mark of a good piece of literature. I have been and am working independently to continuously rehabilitate and grow to become the stronger version of Keli. Of course, I bought the book and brought it to one of our last sessions together. I admittingly cried and was feeling an attachment because he and Dr. Hammel were two massively healing forces that saved my life. Dr. Zelek wrote, "Keep on rolling"!

For continued healing, I was also told to play games such as Luminosity. It's an App that gives you a set of games to play each day and keeps track of your progress. I downloaded the App on my phone and would play additional games and such. Anything to do with numbers, times, memory recall, etc. I have a colleague from work who had a neck injury, and it was severe, which also affected her memory recall. She, too, was playing the same Luminosity App. I had to log back on just to recall exactly what the App does. I laughed because as soon as I loaded it, the first thing it asked me was, "how do you feel today". That's exactly what I was referring to at the beginning of the Neurofeedback sessions and exactly how I begin my testing at work as a Reading Specialist. It even asked me how many hours of sleep I got last night. It flashed a visual memory of Dr. Zelek and Dr. Hammel asking me about my past week's sleeping patterns. I clicked on the answers, and immediately, a game called "lost in migration" popped up, and I giggled. This game measures selective attention. "The ability to focus on relevant information while ignoring the irrelevant distractions". All of the energy I had from playing this game just flashed to me. I just texted a screenshot to my friend, who also played this while rehabilitating. It's certainly not funny, but I cannot believe that I was not able to remember this game that I laid in bed playing for hours, days, weeks, and months. A flock of birds appears on the screen. You have to swipe in the direction that the middle bird is facing. The rest of the birds will be going in a different direction, but the player's job is to focus solely on what the middle bird is doing. (Cracking up and thinking of my mother because she and I lovingly gave each other the bird as a joke). I just played it, and it brought back so many memories. The next game is "pet detective working on problem solving/planning. It states "the process of evaluating options than choosing the best course of action". I wish there was a game like this for my love life. There's my humor coming out, talking about my traumatic experiences and what I did to survive. My humor and desire for love are what gets me through every part of the hard situations I have had to face. There is a game called "word snatchers" to practice "the ability to understand and use words". It gives you a scrambled word on the bottom and a meaning on the top. First, you read the definition of the word and then unscramble the word as fast as you can. It tracks the assigned games for the day with the progress being tracked. Money was well spent in my experience, and when I just played it again, I can advise that it was helpful, and I did enjoy playing the games even during the frustrating points. I was doing everything and anything I could to heal and rehabilitate.

While I was attending the Neurofeedback and playing mental workout games, I was also going to massage therapy almost every week with Diane Ryan, who is a licensed massage therapist and Aesthetician at One Body Spa, who is ridiculously well-versed in healing. She is so knowledgeable and talented, mixed with just being a wonderful soul. As stated directly on their website, "One Body Spa is a privately owned day spa in the beautiful Shawangunk Mountains. We are situated on a private road, surrounded by nature, in a quiet and peaceful setting; we are very close to several excellent Bed and Breakfast Inns, hiking on gorgeous mountain trails, swimming in an invigorating mountain stream, antique shops, cross-country skiing, and fantastic restaurants from casual to elegant. Our goal is to nurture the body to bring balance, comfort, relaxation, and peace to enhance the quality of your life. We have personalized services to help your individual requirements, so you are always given the attention that your one body needs".

Included in these therapies at One Body Spa was cranial sacral still point therapy. This therapy can be done fully clothed for comfort. Diane has shared a resource by Upledger Institute for finding a Cranial Sacral therapist (upledger.com), as they keep an updated list of graduates and can refer people trained by them in their geographic area. All of the visits were documented and given to insurance. I have a unique situation where part of the services did get covered by insurance for a period of time. Then I would pay for the visits and be reimbursed because a script was written by my overseeing doctor. It was a unique twist in my insurance carrier from work. That reimbursement only existed at that time during the first two years of rehabilitation while the court case was still pending. Currently, I go once a month to maintain the same way I see my psychologist once a month for maintenance. Cranial sacral therapy is defined as a gentle hands-on treatment that may provide relief from a variety of symptoms, including headaches and neck pain. Cranial sacral therapy uses a light touch to examine membranes and the movement of fluids in and around the central nervous system. I have been seeing Diane for massages for years before the accident. That was truly a benefit, and I made sure to keep returning to her. She was already aware of my body and anything that I needed in regard to massage beforehand. She even knew about allergies that I previously had. My first visits were also somewhat traumatizing to her to feel and see the pain I was going through physically and emotionally because she is such a compassionate healer. I immediately asked for cranial sacral therapy, and she included it in some sessions. Keep in mind when I describe this therapy that I am a gifted Empath. I will explain what the sensation was like for me personally. The process is that you lay down facing upwards. She sits behind you and gently holds parts of your head. It basically feels like a soft, gentle touch. The touch is light but with no movement at all. I could see changing colors every time she touched my head. The color of healing is a cross between indigo and magenta for me. As a Reiki Master/healer, I see colors when working with energy.

I knew when seeing those colors while she worked on healing me, I could tell right away this was going to be beneficial to my recovery. I began understanding the colors that I see when healing people and being healed by people during my Reiki training. My spiritual gift was working to establish a vocabulary. It works by showing the same signs, colors, experiences when something is repeated. I'll dive deeper into this in the spiritual awakening chapter. Every time my gifted physical therapist Laura at Nina Silverman's Access Physical Wellness & Therapy center put her hands on me to heal my neck, I would also see this deep purple/indigo/magenta color of healing. With Diane, I had already begun seeing an outline of a man with a brimmed hat leaning on a fence. I could tell it was an older period of time clothing with the clothing he had on. It was dark clothing that would cover all of him. The fence overlooked a farm. His back was always to me. I could only see it as dark outlines like a silhouette. I saw this every single time I went to a healing session, whether it was with Diane or my physical therapist. This is very important to who this was during my spiritual awakening. This man who appeared in my healing visions did end up being connected to me through bloodline, with us never meeting. His name was

Oscar. When my Mom was first getting procedures done before leading to her surgery, we were sitting in a waiting room for a long time. I shared with her my vision of this man in my mind during healing sessions. I described him to her in detail. I also explained that while at my friend's Aunt's party, she, who is also gifted from God, said, "you have a man with you and described him exactly as well. His name is Oscar. Do you know an Oscar"? I said, "I don't, but I will check with my Mother". I know how the spiritual world works. As we sat waiting for Mom's procedure, I described this event to my Mom. As I was doing so, the bracelet I had on my right arm while holding her hand ripped off my wrist and fell to the floor. Mom told me that Oscar was like a Godfather to her. She spoke lovingly of him and remained around both of us for a long period of time until her transition to the other side. I no longer see him in my healing visions.

Immediately during these cranial sacral sessions with Diane, my right eye would stop watering. I had improved vision in my right eye. It took me years to gain vision back on both sides to the extent that I have it now. I feel quite back to normal with the peripheral vision now, which has eliminated a lot of PTSD moments. Honestly, I had grown very tired of flinching so many times in a day over silly things. It's not a fun sensation at all. Sometimes it would take me a few minutes to breathe and settle down in the beginning few years of healing. I have been truly blessed to have people directing me to the right healers during this entire time. I am also blessed that I have a close personal friend who is a Shaman. She, too, had a head injury and healed by doing the energy healing work. She was trained in still point as well. During those healing sessions when I saw her for clearing sessions, she would incorporate the still point as well. I also use this with close friends and family members, and it's effective every single time in my experiences when giving and receiving still-point therapy.

My type of personality is "I'm all in" when I know I have to get something done. Healing from this brain injury was an absolute must, and time is of the essence when healing a head injury. I have heard all of their stories and shared mine. The first two years are extremely important for the initial recovery process. I have met, friended, and worked with, in general, 7 people (not including myself or my father) who have suffered from a head injury. We compared accidents, injuries, therapies, and such to how to heal from this. I'm not only well versed in how I healed, but I also know actions others have taken to try to heal from this.

During one of my spiritual cleansing and healing sessions, I was guided by what I refer to as one of my angel friends to see a local osteopathic doctor. I had 13-14 people

I was seeing on the regular during this time to heal as quickly as possible, leaving minimal damage to my body and health. My angel friend Karen, who I'll elaborate on in the spiritual awakening chapter, was able to tell me the name of a local doctor near me. She lives about 4 hours away from me and was doing this on the fly, so to speak. Imagine my surprise when I Googled this man and came up with Dr. Ari Rosen's D.O. In Stone Ridge, NY. He is a doctor who specializes in Osteopathic Manipulative Medicine, Cranial Osteopathy, and Biodynamic Osteopathy. Karen was already able to tell me in detail what he would be able to do and the medical benefits of doing so. I had absolute trust in what she was relaying to me from her personal angels and immediately added his services to my healing team. I just want to remind you that I already had a roster of 14 specialists in every direction working on my right side (neck, shoulder, left side midway near hip down my left leg, left pointer finger, treatments for my head injury, and PTSD). Adding Dr. Rosen was a unique and non-covered expensive service, but I knew the benefits were worth every dollar and minute of time I had. I saw him once a month. I noticed a huge difference in the ability to remain calmer for longer periods of time and was able to sleep well after his sessions. As a matter of fact, it was very much like the sensation of cranial sacral still point therapy. Music would be played as you lay down on your back, facing upwards. He sat behind me and held my head, and gently applied the lightest touch and pressure in different ways. Just like the Neurofeedback, he would ask me how I felt before seeing him and after seeing him each time. Often and I say almost every visit, he would begin his session, and before I knew it, the hour was up. I had been in a deep sleeping state the whole time. I truly, with all of my heart, believe in healing energy work. I remember sharing this information with one of the evaluators for the insurance company (whether or not to continue to cover the cost of my Neurofeedback), and he said, “please don’t be taken advantage of. There is no proven success to this type of treatment, and I don’t want you wasting your time”. I responded, “with all due respect, that's like telling someone not to have religious beliefs. You do you, and I’ll worry about my own energy healing work because I’ve made decisions outside of what the medical field has told me to do, and I absolutely, with all of my heart, know it helped me heal.”

Chapter 4

I have woven in and out of my trauma experiences, giving you episodes of having PTSD, but this is the chapter that I will find the most difficult to write. This chapter is only going to give you short glimpses of what PTSD can look like functionally in the world. One week after my accident, I was just laying in bed for days on end, trying to forget the amount of pain I was in my ex-husband, and I decided to watch a movie. Well, we attempted to watch a movie as it was difficult at that time for me to spend long periods of time watching TV, but I still tried while zoning in and out at times. We were watching a scene where a female casually said goodbye to her spouse, gave a kiss, got in the car, and pulled away to have it get t-boned. I literally sat up in the bed and let out a giant scream. I am not typing this for dramatic effect. It literally triggered a scream of terror because it was unexpected and brought me right to my own trauma. It was this weaving in and out of triggers until they disappear that I am attempting to describe to help others.

Let's begin with the obvious PTSD from the accident, which is self-explanatory, but we have to state it to start this list. I'm not even sure I can put this in a neat chronological order for you to follow. What you will understand from this is the depth of the dark place that I was in emotionally. I was fighting for my life to get back to a balanced and happy emotional state of existence which took years of diligence to my health with experts in the field of therapy to save me. Initially, the first PTSD issues were pain management and depression. This level of depression from losing my identity from a brain injury caused a high-functioning depression for me. I sought out help immediately from Dr. Hammel, my amazing psychologist. With his help, I was able to keep the level of depression within range with diligent calming/ breathing techniques, communication, and whatever exercise I could do at the time to de-escalate.

My first experience with this level of PTSD was from the actual car accident itself. I'll describe the second part of PTSD that started to appear from the actions of other people around me after the accident. I was hit by a drunk driver who was a retired New York Police Detective. I live in a small town that I was not raised in. However, he had plenty of local friends. I lived on a quiet roundabout set of streets. You have to really want to be in my neighborhood to be in it if you can get what I'm saying. I had lived in this house at this point already during the years 2004-2014, so I knew who lived where and who was always walking around the blocks, etc. I was already aware of my surroundings from early childhood experiences, let alone as a person who lived in that small town neighborhood.

Right after the accident, and I mean the following week, older men started coming to my door for various reasons. Some were asking if I was registered to vote (yes, I was already registered). Some would go to all of my neighbors' houses, talk to them and then just leave. I had the same man with a baseball hat and glasses come to my home a few times, trying to ask questions. I knew something wasn't right. Not only am I aware of my surroundings but surrounding energies as well as part of my spiritual gift. During a local Fourth of July parade after the accident, I saw this same man marching with the retired police portion of the parade. I had even taken photos of him at my neighbor's house as proof. I called the police for help. The officer that I was speaking to acted very polite and kind after reporting to him that I had people stop in front of the house and take pictures. I had already shared how small this section of homes is, so we knew everything. Something odd that also happened was suddenly all the houses just around me were getting large amounts of work done that had gone unbothered for 10-12 years; new roofs, solar panels, new driveways, spending a week on the road fixing something all lined up. It was just odd that after so much silence for so many years, it suddenly seemed like New York City while giant Insurance companies and "local friends" checked me out. I have not been silent about any of this I have shared every single event with my psychologist. I would go to the gym (as I was instructed and scripted to go for rehabilitation) and would have people stand directly in front of me with their cell phones facing me, recording me. I refer to these people as "ghosts" because they knew they should not say or do anything that could be used or deemed as a threat. Knowing the full extent to which they are allowed to harass you, they would silently come right up to you and just take photos or record. I get that some people have tried to play the system, but I was not one of them. It made me so paranoid that I would buy a bottle of water every time I left, so I had an arrival time (swiping my tag) and an exit time with the receipt. This is not just PTSD, and this is also someone who is trained to document situations for a living. Going back and looking into these documents, I giggled at the extreme details I kept. Not only did I have the receipts, but I also wrote on each one the distance I was able to complete on the elliptical, the speed, and the calories burned. The calories were important to me because, with the immobility and pain management, I was not able to move as much, which caused weight gain. My insurance paparazzi saw me doing this brief exercise sporadically but didn't see me lying in my bed the rest of the 24-hour day.

I was already warned by a colleague how deep people would go, and private insurance companies will try to catch you faking. This person was well-versed in what happens during court cases and such. Prepared I was and documented everything. I was aware of them trying to do this but was unwilling to stop my healing process at the same time. If anything, I truly wanted my life back. I wanted to go back to teaching. Nothing was going to stop me from being able to walk properly again, let alone be the runner that I am today. That came with diligence and painstakingly determined effort. At that time, being placed under surveillance by many, I kept all receipts, dates, and times and journaled wherever I went. For a period of time, I would say about half a year after the accident, my family and friends couldn't understand the level of harassment I was receiving from all of this surveillance. Then when people started hanging with me in public and seeing the things that I saw, they had to admit that something did seem to be going on. It was difficult for me to even convince my ex-husband at the time that this was happening. It was only when he was with me when things occurred did he start to understand what I had been complaining about. Feeling triggered while begging for help and receiving none because, according to the law, nothing could be done. Why couldn't I get help? You know I checked thoroughly. They are allowed to record, take pictures, speak, or do whatever in public domains as long as they do not pose a credible threat. Then we wonder why people have breakdowns. This is not what I believe in human nature. I'm an energetic alchemist who believes the true reason we are all here is to learn the ways of love. It's bad enough being in a court case, but I knew because of who it was and the nature of this case, I better cross my t's and dot my i's.

I've been seeing Dr. Hammel since shortly after the accident, so we are well into eight and a half years of healing sessions together. I can honestly say that I wouldn't have made it to where I am, which is emotionally balanced, without his guidance. He not only guided me through this PTSD nightmare after the car accident and TBI, but he also guided me through the consistent stress of being a power of attorney for two parents dying at the same time. He guided me through the actual trauma of becoming an instant orphan, with both of them dying 36 hours apart during the pandemic of 2020. Then after that, I had the divorce selling my home, and starting over again. He has been witness to me entering the dating world clumsily. He has literally been the foundation of my emotional balance. I didn't have to re-explain anything. I could vent and cry to him, and at times he would coddle me. At other times would tell me to knock it off. It's so comforting, especially now with my parents gone and no romantic partner to turn to for support. I've had to navigate this alone, but I can honestly say that Dr. Hammel has been there providing the healing maintenance needed to not just survive but live.

For his services, the evaluations came from conversations, observations, and a questionnaire that determines the level of anxiety or PTSD. He is the actual doctor that completes the paperwork for my 504 at work each year. I would not have made it without him, which I openly shared with him. I made jokes about being called a "wild black beauty" by him years ago. We can even giggle about past arguments for the benefit of me growing as an independently happy person. The world has truly blessed me with excellent, talented healing professionals, and Dr. Hammel is certainly one of them. Nothing but respect and adoration there, for sure. I had to be extremely independent, but during these traumas, I got a little emotionally lost. With an extremely sympathetic approach, he helped me to be in the mindset to not make the worst of things and make the best of things during these traumas. He got me to stop looking for outside validation to heal myself. Other people couldn't be the reason I would start feeling better, and I decided that I had to rehabilitate myself. In that, I felt freedom and fought hard. I was also making sure that I could continue to be the best Mom possible for my son. He was a driving force in my rehabilitation.

One of the first things I did to make sure I demonstrated to him that I would still be his Mom was to create memories. I finally took him to Disney World. I was so traumatized, even before the rest of my other traumas were about to unfold, that life could just disappear in the blink of an eye. I was determined to live in the moment while constantly trying to keep myself out of the past.

Disneyland was exhilarating and difficult at the same time. I couldn't walk much or for long periods of time. We bought speed passes, but I still had to use a wheelchair. Do you know how challenging that was to maneuver in Disney World? I had a doctor's note and was able to have a special notice about my PTSD. Not only did we go in the speed pass line, but we were not held for long periods of time because I would start to get high levels of anxiety if I had massive amounts of people close to me or with multiple loud sounds. Not the best place for someone like this, right? I was one determined Mother, and my ex-husband did a great job making sure people surely got the heck out of our way. It made me think of my parents when my Dad would push my Mom into the wheelchair. He made no exceptions to anyone. It was an "I'm coming and move before I run you over" approach, and I felt myself constantly putting my foot down to try and stop him. I can also see a flashback of my mother doing the same action, so when it happened to me, I was amused yet not amused simultaneously.

Some of the rides were fun, but I would suffer greatly in pain later. It didn't matter because my nine-year-old at the time was living his best life even though I was in a wheelchair. I was also heavily medicated to try and numb the physical pain. He got hip to the situation and, on the Aladdin ride, yelled out to a guy, "My Mom is handicapped". I got upset and said, "Please don't do that, son. It's obvious right now, and it makes me feel bad". Later on that day, I even tried to have a sense of humor about it. At Universal, they wanted us to write my name and place it on the plastic on the wheelchair, so it was labeled when I left the wheelchair at the gates. I saw my son and ex-husband cracking themselves up writing something. When they turned around, it was a minion, and it said "Handi-Kane" instead of handicapped. I did laugh, and I still have that label from the chair. Life goes on, right? On the second trip to Disney World, I decided to have mercy on my ex-husband and rented a motorized scooter. It was still difficult battling light exposure, sound sensitivity, and hypervigilance with people all around.

During the years of psychology sessions, Dr. Hammel changed his office location three times. The second move was in a place that coincidentally happened to be around the corner from the restaurant that "he", the drunk driver, hung out in all the time. I am calling him "he" because this is not a personal attack on him directly. I am a healer, and believe it or not, I do not judge. Absolutely I was angry as hell for about six years at least, and then I could finally just let it go. I'd say that once I had to refocus solely on my dying parents, I just let go of that anger because I had no room for it. I had to just get to a place of forgiveness. These traumas were done. Consequences were paid. Life moves on. I'm simply stating the intense PTSD that was occurring in the first few years to help others navigate through this and also feel comfort knowing that this is a period of time. Yes, it takes a long period of time, but it can be healed and forgiven. Please keep in mind that I didn't skip a beat with my healing sessions with Dr. Hammel. You can't expect results without putting in the hard work to heal. The third time Dr. Hammel relocated his office, it was directly across the street from this restaurant. One time "he" stood outside in front with a plaid shirt staring directly at me as I entered the office to see Dr. Hammel. I was beside myself. The whole day had gone well, but the moment I saw him, I was instantly triggered and frustrated. Dr. Hammel made sure to walk outside with me to make sure I was fine getting into the car to go. Every time after that, I was always nervous about going to my sessions and would sprint from my car into the building, never looking back each time.

There were a few times when I would be out in public, and "he" would come right up alongside me and say nothing.

He would just stand there and observe. This happened a few times, and each time he did this, I reported it to my lawyer and psychologist. My first lawyer and I had filed for a protection order. First, I was told that they didn't know where he was staying at the time. Then I was told that they couldn't honor the protection order. Not sure why that happened, but as I keep repeating, I always suspected things were handled a little differently for this man. In his mind, he thought I was fine. He must not have believed that whatever was happening to him should have happened. I even got myself into a frenzy, questioning if it was actually him or not. My Mom was alive at the time of these calls, and she could tell by my voice and description (and she was also spiritually gifted) that most of these times, it was truly him. Can I prove it? No, I didn't care to stop and take his photo. I will tell you this as someone who has suffered multiple traumas, and that is you do not forget a face when something or someone has wounded you this deeply.

The "tailing" by "ghosts," is what I called them, was four agencies deep. I had my insurance company checking to make sure I wasn't faking. I had the drunk driver's insurance company following me to make sure I wasn't faking. I had private investigators from the drunk driver's lawyer, his local friends, and his retired buddies all checking on me. Meanwhile, I'm being watched to the point of harassment and couldn't get any help at all. The local police officer acted very nice to my face and told me to send him the information that I had, and he would do his best to see who was coming around me.

I'm trained to notice what wouldn't be noticed in my line of work. I'm also a gifted person, so I feel things before they're coming. Matched with actual companies coming close to me, recording me everywhere I was going. It was a nightmare. I noticed out-of-state license plates (rental cars) around me everywhere I went. In this small town I had rarely seen one before. During my court case, there were plenty everywhere I went. I had cars always sitting on my local routes on the sides of the roads with hazard lights on. These cars were sitting in places that I had never seen cars sitting in the 11 years I had lived there so far at that time. They were always in crazy spots and quite often dangerously sitting there. Some of the cars with flashing hazard lights would pull out behind me as soon as I passed. It's been almost nine years since the accident, and this still happens in big bursts once in a while and then disappears again. Back during the court case, I would call my Mother in PTSD fashion, frustrated each time. Since I called her each time, we both noticed the pattern. The "tailing" would be the strongest after an evaluation or right before there was a new development with the court case or coverage of a new set of appointments.

Sometimes this would happen three times in a 52-minute drive to work. I confided all of this to the seemingly helpful officer. I can't recall the exact day, but the sky was dusk. I have the emails that I had sent to this seemingly helpful officer still in my personal emails. In 2015 this officer brought two doctors to my front door wearing classic white long coats. I immediately started yelling at them all. I couldn't believe the antics that were happening, only proving to me that this was all related to who this person was and not the incident itself. My ex-husband went to the door and talked to the officer while I was trying to call my lawyer. He wouldn't answer my phone, but he called my ex-husband. Now I'm more upset than ever. I had already been diagnosed with PTSD and had been in therapy for a long time. I also explained to the doctors that the officer acted like he was going to help me. They left unhappy with the officer. They verbally stated, "Why did you bring us here if you knew she was already in therapy services". Obviously, they were covering themselves for this traumatic situation. I was sure to inform my psychologist. I switched lawyers after this incident.

We had already had the restitution hearing, which was a nightmare in itself. I was crying so hard I was offered a chance to leave the stand and regain my composure in the back room. The person who was on guard at the time told me, “I think what you are doing is extremely brave”. I was thinking, “Who the hell is this person”? All I knew was that a few weeks prior, I was offered money to not follow through with going to the restitution hearing. I was not having that at all and demanded a hearing. I wanted to say what I needed to say. This was not the major court case yet, but I was going to state publicly what happened. Everyone wanted me to be hush-hush about this, and that simply wasn’t going to happen. Whether this is the typical situation where lawyers work around things or whether it was different because of who this was didn’t matter to me. My story was going to be told. I filled out an application for public access to records on June 27, 2014, twenty days after the car accident. I received a statement from the Police Department regarding my FOIL request “the - Police Department is in receipt of your FOIL request. Unfortunately, I must inform you that we are not able to complete your present request at this time. The reason for this denial is that this case has not yet been adjudicated through the courts. Pursuant to Pittari v. Pirro, [258 Ad2d 202 (1999)], these files are excluded as part of investigative files until such time as the case has been adjudicated. If the - Police Department can be of any further service to you, please do not hesitate to contact my office”. I figured, okay, I understand the case was still in motion. My only thought was to see what he was actually charged with and what happened on his end as I was fighting for my life to rehabilitate. Did he lose his license? Did any charges even get filed? His alcohol content was .436. That's not a “Whoopsies”. When I started writing this book, I came across this paper and got dressed and went back over again, and applied for a FOIL request on December 8, 2022. I also provided a copy of the previous request and a denial letter. December 12, 2022, I received an electronic email stating, “Dear Ms. Kane. The - Police Department is in receipt of your FOIL application, and this communication serves to acknowledge your request as per statute. Please be advised that due to the current high volume of FOIL applications received by this agency, there will be a delay in processing your request. Your application is now in the queue, and you will receive a more detailed response shortly. On January 10, 2023, I received an email with the attached requested report form. It was the first time that the true wording from the account of my witnesses from the accident was shared with me. I cannot recall how much information I was actually given from my lawyers at the time. You need to remember that I was on the brink of a traumatic brain injury suffering from serious PTSD. I will give everyone the benefit of the doubt, but I truly don’t believe that what I read was stated to me at any time. At no time did my lawyers read the statement to me verbatim. I think that was an important healing step missed by them. However, that was not their goal at the time. It’s mine. So here was what was printed on the report. After seeing what I have shared and I chose not to alter anything in my account after receiving this report. It's important to see all sides of the story. The report stated, "Markings and struck NY Reg D##-#### operated by Kane. Kane had already exited her vehicle and was laying along roadside and being attended to by Diaz Ambulance and Fire Department. Member did observe… (Him, I added this, but I still won't type his name. This is not about him; this is about how to maneuver and heal from this). Member did observe (him) at the driver's wheel of his vehicle. Upon attempting to approach the vehicle was approached by witnesses who had secured a bottle of vodka which she stated she observed (him) take one swig from before she removed it from him and stated that another witness, Penney, had taken his keys as he was also attempting to leave the scene. Upon approaching (him) in his vehicle, a strong odor of alcohol was emanating from his vehicle. When the member spoke to him, he responded in slurred speech, and the member did observe the glassy eyes of the subject. The subject stated, "I screwed up, I'm sorry". Member instructed the subject to get out of his vehicle but, due to the collision, could not exit the driver's door. Member also observed very impaired motor skills as the subject attempted to climb over the center console to exit the passenger side. Upson reaching the passenger seat (he), sat in the seat, and passed out briefly and repeatedly. Upon these actions, the member requested an additional ambulance for (him). Upon the arrival of the Mobile Life Unit, 228 subjects were cared for by EMS personnel and also advised he was under arrest although he was in and out of consciousness. The subject was transported by mobile life ambulance to Kingston Hospital, where he was admitted through the ER. Once at Kingston Hospital ER at 11:55 AM, HRS (he) was read his DWI warning and refused a blood test. He was read Miranda warning at 11:56 AM hrs. At 12:22 hrs. (He) was read DWI warning a second time and agreed to a blood test. At that time, stating, "Yes, I will submit to the chemical test". This was witnessed by ER tech (blocking name), who was treating (him) at the time. At 12:37 hrs. blood test was drawn by (a man), and samples were secured at that time by this member. The subject was then cared for more by ER personnel while this member prepared tickets and a DWI Bill of Particulars. Upon returning to his room (he) was issued UTT for 1192-3 A fail to keep right and also a DWI bill of particular released to hospital personnel upon issuance of tickets for further extended care by the hospital, and the member turned to service." I also received communication from the Captain on January 10, 2023, that "the operator of the vehicle was charged with aggravated DWI and failure to keep right. He pled guilty in "full satisfaction of all other charges; he paid a fine and was sentenced to probation." This information set my soul free because what I was reporting was indeed what happened, yet I was brutally questioned again and again and again like this wasn't all documented. It does set me free, knowing that this was a game of money and accountability and that they knew I was telling the truth about my experiences. It still didn't stop the shady tailing from happening to me and some other shady scenarios.

Jumping to the past again, I received a letter from the County Office of the District Attorney on July 21, 2014, stating that in the Case of People v. "he". I'm keeping the name private on purpose. It's a public record, but this is not about him. This is about the healing process, but it was different from the others because of who "he" was. It stated, "Dear Ms. Kane. I have been assigned to handle the above matter arising from an incident.... I would like to schedule a time to meet with you about this case. If you wish to have your civil attorney present, please have him/her call me". I met with him alone. I had nothing to hide and was honest and direct about what happened. Later on, I was told things were postponed because he was no longer taking the case. I don't remember the rationale I was given, but along with other things, I had my own suspicions. Thinking to the present time reflecting on this information and experiencing PTSD, I can only imagine his line of work must have also caused PTSD. He was, in my opinion handling it incorrectly. This is exactly what I was trying to avoid during my healing recovery from this accident. I was not perfect and sure had my share of wine while crying and mourning over the loss of myself. The only thing he did terribly wrong was endangering himself and failing to call for help instead of putting my life (or anyone else's) at risk. You don't get to a capacity to be at a .436 alcohol content and be alive without already having experience in drinking. He knew he needed help. He should have gotten it.

I had to change lawyers after the arrival of the doctors with the police officer on my lawn. I no longer trusted him since he failed to communicate with me that night. This was simply not going to work. A new lawyer was recommended who had experience defending traumatic brain injury cases. He is incredibly talented, and I brought my MRI' and everything to him, and he was able to decipher everything. He accepted my case, and I hired him. He told me to call my lawyer, and I got so nervous that he decided to make the call with me present. My first lawyer tried to tell him, "You don't really know what's going on here". Still, to this day, I'm not really sure what he personally was referring to, and it makes me upset even thinking of it. Regardless, we made the change. Yes, it complicated things, but nothing has to remain the way it is. There is always a way to change, even if it's an incredibly difficult task. I was thrilled that I changed lawyers. There was only one time he called aggressively, stating that I didn't share something with him. I pushed back hard because I was emotionally exhausted with insurance, doctors, lawyers, and supposed friends not believing what I was saying in regard to the depths of my injuries. I knew how brutally injured I was, and the lengths that companies will fight to make sure money is not paid is ridiculous. Meanwhile, this court case was considered "No Fault". I was not able to sue him civilly. The only money that came out of this was the difference between his insurance coverage and mine. He only paid $700 during the restitution hearing. He didn't have to pay anything, and it was the insurance company. By the time you paid the lawyers the fee for defending you, a little over one year's salary for me was the compensation for the trauma and suffering I endured/endured at times and permanent lifetime management of this. There was even a phone call asking me to accept less, just like the phone call I received to drop the restitution hearing and accept less. I said "no" to dropping the case and settling. I was told doing this could lock me into a long case and possibly lose all financial help. I said to them, "I want the truth told. I am not backing down". They ended up going with the set amount my lawyer stated. All of this stress was happening while I was trying to make it to my 3-4 therapies a day, trying to raise my 7-year-old son, and keep some sanity in my marriage. I will say that I am so lucky and truly grateful that included in this were the costs of my rehabilitation. I made the swift move to go to as much therapy as possible and rehabilitate immediately, and those costs were covered. I consider that alone God's gift in a horrible situation.

Pain management is another beast that belongs to PTSD. My wild black beauty spirit wanted to be my old self (karate, roller-blading, jumping on bounce houses with my young son, etc.) so bad that I would push myself to collapse to the floor while trying to clean or do dishes. Dr. Hammel gave me the book The Pain Survival Guide: How to Reclaim Your Life, written by Dennis C. Turk, Ph.D., and Frits Winter, Ph.D., to read. He giggled when I showed up with highlighted sections and notes written directly on the pages and posted them to hold certain places in the books. He said," I should have known when I asked a Reading Specialist to read this while smirking." This is certainly a far cry from our initial appointments. He taught me how to maneuver from my usual state of "I need to get everything done now" to "well, I can only get one thing done at a time". This was not an easy transition physically and especially not emotionally for me.

In the beginning of my healing sessions with Dr. Hammel, I was angry at everything that was happening, mixed with confusion due to a TBI while experiencing

PTSD. I was in excruciating pain while trying to heal, with judgment flying from every insurance company possible. Often I would be sent to the farthest places ever to have an evaluation that insurance was making me go to in order to have continued services. Many of these places made me nervous to even go to. The doctors would seem compliant and listen and seemingly side with you. Then the report would come to discredit you so money would not have to be paid, and I would be in a rage for weeks. There is one thing I cannot stand, and that is lying. In general, in all areas of my life, I am a truth-teller. This insurance game because that's what it was starting to feel like was upsetting me to a PTSD point. It got to the point where Dr. Hammel asked me to come to him with the reports instead of reading them alone anymore.

I recall a particularly heavy day when I was so enraged at what was happening to me. Just like I was venting to Dr. Zelek about "wanting my life back" and "how much longer do I have to wait to see the final damage that I'm left with". When Dr. Hammel told me four years, my PTSD lit up, and I was wild, crying and yelling and just infuriated. I was even mad at him for saying it would take four years. It blew my mind, and I was wild. Dr. Hammel called me a "wild black beauty". For those of you who have followed me on any social media platforms I am on (Instagram, Facebook,

Twitter, and TikTok), that's why I did the photoshoot with the gorgeous black horse. I wrote the caption, "This photo has a deep spiritual meaning to me. Eight years ago, when my psychologist initially told me how long it would take to recover and possibly never fully recover, I went wild in his office. Screaming, crying, and yelling because I couldn't even speak enough words expressively, and everything was trapped. I was so upset I was going to lose myself over someone else's poor decision. He tried his best to settle me but was guarding me and calling me a "wild black beauty". We laugh about this now. So this is me holding that beauty still. I did it"! Dr. Hammel has done his magic and has saved my life not only through this accident but with the following trauma behind it. He taught me breathing techniques to calm the nervous system when triggered. These breathing exercises are used to minimize the effect of a trigger. There was an App that we downloaded on my phone that I could turn to if I started to feel triggered or sad. Having a brain injury and PTSD causes a lot of fluctuations in moods as well as massive amounts of fatigue.

Of course, I had PTSD in regards to riding in vehicles and still do at times. I feel safer in SUV's. I'll get in Sedans, but I am hyper-vigilant, and it's not the best feeling. One time shortly after the accident, I had a rental car, and it was a sedan. I was not happy about this at all. My ex-husband was driving the car, and a large truck was approaching from behind, slamming on his brakes. While the car was in slow motion forward, I opened the door and was going to jump out. My ex screamed and pulled my ponytail to keep me from getting out of the car, yelling shut the door. It was not pretty. Needless to say, it definitely affected our marriage because he was an aggressive driver, and it always freaked me out. I had this conversation with Dr. Hammel many times. He gave me the advice of sitting in the back with my son if the driving wasn't changing. This would narrow down my response to anyone's aggressive driving techniques.

I've had PTSD trigger responses randomly in the driving world. One time I was on my way to my cranial sacral therapy session. The car directly in front of me slammed into a truck in front of him. It was a road that had a speed limit of 55 mph. I slammed on my brakes and sat struck with fear of what I witnessed. I saw everyone running out of the Audi shop and opening the doors to the sedan. The front of the sedan was smoking. The driver was a male and hopped out and grabbed a baby carrier out of the back seat, and handed it to a bystander who was helping. The female in the front passenger side was not moving. It was like I was watching my own accident. I didn't get out because everyone was already there, and help was already deployed. I put my flashers on and crept a little closer, thinking I'll make sure no other cars approached. Once I had reached my session, I cried, and she was able to help me with the treatment. Another time I was returning from the hospital before the pandemic hit, visiting my parents, and I got stopped right in front of my turn-off on the Thruway. I was sitting behind another giant truck. I couldn't see what was happening, but a Trooper started walking in front of my car. I looked to the right and saw a horse trailer tossed to the far right side way off of the highway. I was thinking, "oh no, I hope the horse is safe," and then, without notice, BOOM. The trooper in front of me had to kill the horse. Unbeknownst to me, the horse was under that truck directly in front of me. Here we go again. I'm in tears recalling this. I let out a ridiculous scream in my car and started sobbing. I called my mother through the car speakers, and she was doing her best to keep me calm so that I could drive safely home. I have shared these stories with Dr. Hammel, and I kept asking, "Why is this happening? I have driven for years, and nothing of this magnitude was happening to me". I was desperate to clear this cycle of what I call "car PTSD" out of my system. I could write almost nine years' worth of examples, but I think whoever is reading this can get the gist of what I'm trying to share here. There are constant triggers in life to traumas that happen to all of us. The work has to be done to keep the triggers and responses down to minimal responses or not be triggered at all. Recently I posted a video stating that I was proud of myself. I was returning home from a massage appointment, and I watched a car come off of a roundabout and drive completely into a car that was in front of me. I slammed on breaks and was looking to see if they were okay. They didn't collide that hard, but I was triggered only to a small extent. This time I was going to call in help or get help. Ten seconds ahead was a trooper sitting in the middle. I pulled right up to him, and he rolled his window down alert. Once he saw it was me, he seemed calmer, but hey, I don't blame his response either. I told him what had happened and who was responsible for the crash. Then I went home. I didn't have any other anxiety about it at all. I was proud of myself.

I didn't get to this point alone. I again reiterate that I have had the most amazing healing professionals helping me. I saw a Neuropsychologist, psychologist, the general doctor overseeing all the doctors that I was seeing, and two different chiropractors. When one of the chiropractors reset my left index finger, I actually cried. It was so painful. It was not in place after the airbags deployed and was sitting on a nerve that kept me awake all night, and all the Percocet in the world would not have stopped it. I saw two hand therapists to gain mobility back in my left index finger. To this day, I no longer hold the steering wheel at "10 and 2" in case of airbags deploy. It actually triggered me to a flashback of how my mother always drove holding the wheel at * and 4. That's what I do now to avoid this injury again if I'm ever in a crash which I hope I am not. I guess that counts as another PTSD trauma. I never want to go through that pain again, either. It's a finger, but I tell you, it was ridiculous pain, and the therapy was quite difficult to manage pain-wise. I saw an orthopedic surgeon who gave me cortisone shots in my shoulders, and that was so excruciating I didn't even breathe when it was given. I couldn't use my arm at all after that for a while. I saw two different physical therapists to address the neck, right shoulder, lower left hip and lower back pain. The pain and struggle just kept rotating issues as I was trying to rehabilitate. I wasn't even walking correctly, and it started to hurt my knee. I saw the Neurosurgeon initially to make sure there was no brain bleeding and such, as I spoke about earlier.

The second chiropractor was the only man to finally stop my left hip lower back pain. He and my massage therapist kept telling me that the pain in my left hip/lower back region radiating pain all the way down my leg was coming from the psoas. My massage therapist, Dianne, would always help keep that taken care of during our sessions. It would be better for the moment and create pain again later as I tried to regain walking strength and endurance. This chiropractor, who has now retired, had sports medicine experience. One day he asked me to lay down facing up. He sat along my left side and leaned over me, saying, "Keli, this is going to hurt, but I promise it's going to help you". He explained his training and experience and put his hand firmly, and even the word firmly doesn't state it on the psoas. Holding it in place (which was already hurting) asked me to lift my left leg. I actually couldn't do it. He was doing his best to cheer me on to lift my leg, and when I did, it was so painful I started to shake and cry at the same time while fighting the pain. I did that a few times and then finally just sat there in shock, trying to calm down. I went home, took pain meds, and got right into the hot tub. I cried in the hot tub as well as calling my mother, explaining the therapy I had just gone to. The next day I didn't have the same level of pain anymore. Literally like I was freed. This was after seeing two different specialists for back pain. They wanted to give me cortisone shots in my back and hip. I knew what that felt like from my shoulder, and I was not thrilled with this idea. I kept up with the massage, physical therapists, and chiropractor because I was determined to try and heal this naturally. This chiropractor and massage therapist saved me because once we narrowed down exactly the spot where all this pain was stemming from, I could get specific help and started walking normally again. This meant less neck, shoulder, and back pain. It affected everything from driving to where I couldn't turn my head fully or even hold my head in the air while driving. I had to lean back a little and have my head leaning on the rest while driving. One time a friend of mine was putting makeup on me, and I couldn't even sit up that long. Just pushing the brush on my face was too much resistance for my neck. I had to lay down for her to put the make-up on. Then, of course, everyone sees me, and I look fine, right? I was just so determined to continue to live in the moment.

Everyone wasn't aware it was a constant and dangerous roller coaster ride of drugs with Percocet, Xanax, Flerxeril, and Naproxen just to be able to fight off the pain in order to function. Cautiously checking each time I take them that nothing interferes with each other. There were times that I was afraid to take a nap (which you need to do a lot to heal from a brain injury) for the fear that I would not wake up. My son was little, so naps made it a challenge because I had to help him stay safe too. It was after my first year of healing that I knew I no longer wanted these drugs in my body, let alone be available in my own home. I had them locked in a safe. Anything could happen, including my naughty puppy at the time, who was eating everything. I decided enough was enough, and with my spiritual training, which I will get into soon in this book, I wanted my body cleared of all toxins as much as possible. I went to Glen R. Finley N.D. at the New Leaf Holistic Health. Taken directly from his website, "Dr. Finley studied pre-med at The University of California at Santa Cruz and earned a Naturopathic Doctorate degree from the National University of Natural Medicine in Portland, Oregon. He has been in private practice since 2001 and co-founded New Leaf Holistic Health in Kingston, NY. Dr. Finley's philosophy is that optimal health begins with digestion and assimilation. He specializes in digestive disorders, detoxification, skin conditions, food allergies, men's and children's health, and enjoys a general family practice." He and his wife are lovely and very talented healers. I knew of him through treating friends of mine. He immediately knew what supplements I needed to take, paying close attention to being able to sleep. He knew it was critical to get these heavy-hitting drugs out of the liver. PTSD also creates cortisone which can wreak havoc on your bodily functions as a whole. I learned a lot from Dr. Finely and still have maintenance visits with him. He was the person who finally got my fight or flight response settling my nervous system. He also taught me to rotate my sleeping remedies. I had to take things on a rotating basis, so my body didn't acclimate to it, rendering it useless to me. I rotated Rescue Remedy, Melatonin, Tryptophan, Tensions Ease, Benadryl, and Valerian. Recently I've included broad-spectrum CBD sleep vegan gummies. Of course, I had to rotate these on a daily for the first few years after the accident, but as time went on, I could start to take them less here and there until I did not need any of these sleep remedies at all. I only take one of these occasionally now. The second most important thing we addressed was the need to enhance my recovery from the traumatic brain injury. For that, I was told to take Phosphatidylserine and other supplements that help the adrenal system function. I highly suggest homeopathy as a means of healing. The hardest medicine for me to get off of was Xanax. I had to find another way of calming, which I learned with my psychologist and spiritual healers.

Chapter 5

Many who are suffering from depression often overlook seeking help for the mental and physical aspects of healing. People know how to heal mentally and physically but often miss healing the spiritual side. The last 8, close to 9 years of my life, would make one hell of a lifetime movie with the traumas I've gone through. This in no way minimizes anyone's pain and suffering. I'm simply a person who dusted off and got back up again several times because I refused to give up on myself. I warn you that as you keep reading, you may experience a sad emotional charge for me.

I'm going to take you through the journey of my spiritual transformation, which has so many paths. I'll begin with who I was as a little girl but was not really allowed to talk about it. When I did talk about it, there was always a mixed reaction. People either were so condemning and afraid they rejected me, or they were so intrigued but also fearful and were close to me but always knew I was "different". I've always had a kind, open heart wanting to help others. It was just in me to be a caretaker and help others. In Kindergarten, I would line up my stuffed animals and teach them something like I was already a classroom teacher. I knew at a very young age exactly where I was going to end up. I'm now a Kindergarten Reading Specialist for the last 5 years specializing in teaching young children with needs how to read. It just demonstrates that I just knew that I was supposed to "teach". I was the type of person that had too many feelings. I channeled everything that had emotion. It was difficult to handle at times. I couldn't throw away paper because I truly believed that anything that existed on the planet had feelings. I partially giggle at this and don't at the same time from my older perspective. I spent a good portion in solitude, where my parents would get concerned and tell my older sister to take me with her. You see, we lived in an extremely active haunted home, and I was the one that it seemed to have most of its focus on. I could hear them, see them, and most of the time, when water was running, they would call out my name. It was horrifying. It would be so loud that I would jump out of the shower, which I'm sure they found amusing, and continued to do this to get a reaction. I've had friends over, and we would call something out, and it would just happen. Honestly, if my friends weren't there with me to witness some of these things, I would have been afraid that I was going crazy. One time my friend and I were already nervous, and we could feel weird energy. The cat was at the front door, and I jokingly called out, "hey ghost let the cat out, will ya'?" This old full glass door with an old difficult-to-turn lock turned and clicked, and my friend Danielle ran from the other side of the room and jumped on my lap. We were terrified. The door slowly slid open. We were frozen in fear for so long. This is only one of the things I had to grow up with that I couldn't share because it was not socially accepted. I had objects moved and hidden from me all the time. My Dad never believed me until one night I was totally asleep. I opened my eyes and saw him standing there, staring at me. I got scared and said, "what are you doing, Dad"? He said, "Why did you do that? What did you need?" I was confused because I didn't do anything. I was fast asleep. He went on to tell me that he heard "me" speak to him and then walk back through the dining room, which had a distinct rattling of china when anyone crept through. I did sleep and walk a lot when I was younger, and I never knew what I did at all ever. I now wonder if that was something a little more than just "sleepwalking" because as soon as I left that house, it never happened to me again. So Dad just figured I was sleepwalking but quickly figured out that it wasn't me and started to finally understand that, yes, indeed, there was a haunting going on in that home. It was really hard for my Dad to accept this was happening. He always knew my Mother had the "spiritual gift", and knew I was also "different," but we weren't allowed to really talk about it because, like I keep saying, it was a taboo subject at the time.

I was never harmed, just always afraid literally of my own shadow because I knew when I was home, I was going to interact with them one way or the other. I told family members, and although my sister lovingly called me weird, it was still frowned upon at that time to discuss what was happening to me. My Mom and Dad were very hard-working individuals who were always at work. They had to have no other choice, money had to be made. They didn't work one job either; they both had multiple jobs. I did my best to stay in the lane to get where I wanted in life, but there were many school events in that I didn't have anyone present to see me. They did what they could when they could, and I accepted this. It's just demonstrating that while understanding that I was different, there always seemed to be some sort of circumstance that would also make me even more "different".

I had/have a very good personality and loved/love helping people, so I had no problem making friends inside the school building. I was always in the "popular crowd". I grew up with two sets of twin best friends. One set was Karra and Camille in my elementary years, and the other set was Tamara and Theresa in my middle school beginning of High School years. I'm mentioning them because somehow I always seem to be friends or be around sets of twins. These sets of twins did accept my unique gifts and were very protective friends over me. I cherish all the memories I made with them. So while all of this was going on for me, I had little guardians watching after me making sure I was alright, mixed in with a lot of fun memories.

I'm going to skip straight ahead, leaving so many spiritual happenings unspoken to get to the root of my healing after the car accident. I'll talk about the home that I lived in while I was married and was there from the years 2004-2022. A few months after moving into the home, I started having more paranormal activities happening, particularly in the room which was used as a storage/office area. Anytime I went in there, I always felt uneasy. I felt heavily watched at all times. I've been "touched," meaning tapping or even had scratches. All the praying in the world and holy water wasn't working. It was something my ex-husband didn't understand, even though he could see these things that would speak to me right in front of him or see the scratches left. I will just say that my son, although he does his best to ignore it, does seem to have the same family lineage spiritual gift as me. A mixture of things that happened in life and how it's now sometimes socially accepted to speak of the other side, he has a brilliant open mind. I am truly blessed to have such a genuinely kind soul for a son. The point of this is to show that there was already activity in my home before my car accident. I am briefly trying to describe years of living with a gift (which felt like a curse) for years without understanding how to protect, clear, and use my gift. All of this has already been happening for my entire life, and it didn't matter where I lived, it was always active. I would get so upset, and my sister always yelled, "It's YOU", it's not where you are. This always made me mad because I was like, "what's wrong with me then" and I would get very emotional. I prayed, lived a moral life, always helping others, and did what I was supposed to do in society, and I couldn't understand why these things always found me.

Here came the accident, and my life was turned upside down ever further. Now I'm trapped at home, laying in bed with an inability to do anything really except suffer (all the Percocet in the world and muscle relaxers were not relinquishing me of this pain). I looked up the churches in the area and joined The Reformed Church of Saugerties. I went there one time and sat in mass, and I truly loved the style and delivery of Pastor Terry. His wife was an actual Broadway actress, and the music/choir was just magical. This is my first step in my spiritual healing. I joined and brought my son and ex-husband there. My son loved it there; he was only seven years old at the time. It always bothered me that I didn't baptize my son. I truly believed in saving and guarding the soul. My ex-husband didn't agree or disagree, and it just was what it was. He's not an atheist, but just not a spiritual person, either. I was so concerned and fixated on getting my son baptized at the time. I remember sitting there thinking, "what I died that day"? What were they going to do with my body? Did they even know that I wanted to be cremated? I do not want my body stuck in the ground. I want my ashes set free because ashes to ashes and dust to dust. My soul will already be where it needs to be; this body is only a shell. So my brilliant idea was to protect both of them and have them baptized at the same time, having a spiritual Daddy/Son bonding experience. This made my heart so very happy.

During this same time frame, almost nine years ago, I befriended a person who was studying Shamanism under my personal Shaman and dear sweet friend, who I also call family at this point, Barbara-Jean. I was explaining my whole life history with spirits and such, and this newly studying Shaman was doing her best to clear my energy but needed to refer to Barbara-Jean to help because she realized how serious my situation was. I would not be able to heal properly if I couldn't even be at ease in my own home. Adding to that trauma, suffering in pain, sadness, and stress energy to myself, who was gifted with drawing energy towards me for years. Barbara-Jean helped me with healing sessions and a house clearing to live in a blessed home on protected land. Barbara-Jean is trained by the Four Winds Society and holds their degree as certified in the Light Body School of Luminous Healing and Energy Medicine. She has personally studied under the Societies' Founder, Alberto Villodo. She had also studied in Head and Spine Trauma through the American Polarity under Roger Gilchrist and holds a certificate as an Associate Practitioner. The first thing Barbara-Jean did was clear the energy in my home and seal off any portals of entering and exiting for energies. This is where Barbara-Jean entered my life and saved my soul, teaching me what I need to know to protect myself and my family. She told me to take my pets out of my home and remove all mirrors from home. Still, to this day, no mirrors are kept in our bedrooms. The mirror I have in my home have mirrors glued to the backs of them facing the wall, or they have been "shut down" as I have been trained to do by my friend Patti. The animals were removed to protect them during this blessing of the home. My spiritually naive self was thinking, "oh my gosh, this is a bit dramatic," but I couldn't refuse. I was willing to try anything to heal and finally be set free into positivity and white light energy. I did as she asked. I could feel intuitively this was the right path.

I've always had sensitivities to mirrors. I had inherited an old family mirror, and I never felt right while it was in the house. It was in the attic, but I listened to Barbara-Jean and took it out. I actually had my ex-husband destroy it and get rid of it because I didn't want someone else bringing that energy into their home. At this time, I learned about mirrors being portals which made immediate sense to me. I was so afraid of many mirrors, and that's because I could sense and feel which ones were active. Of course, I never spoke about this unless you were family or a very close friend because many don't understand this.

Barbara-Jean and I had prepared a statement about what I wanted to bring into the home's atmosphere. What quality of life did I want to have there? Who was welcome in the home, and who was not? Right before she came to my house, and I mean minutes before, with my animals out of the house (cats and dogs), I was walking from that spooky office to my bedroom, and right behind me were the heavy footsteps of a tall spirit right behind me. I could feel the vibration of the steps under my bare feet on the hardwood floor. My heart almost stopped. I turned around and walked out the front door waiting for Barbara-Jean to arrive. Whoever was there knew that some cleansing was going to happen. I was anxious for her to pick up a vibe in the backyard. There was a spot right off of my deck where five different dogs dug relentlessly, making a giant pit that I had to buy dirt to fill in. I blessed it with holy water and everything, and they always went directly out the back door to that spot and dug. When I yelled for them to stop, they would lay right on top of it. She came to my home with the preparation completed to capture the Earth-bound entities. She cleared the home and completed a blessing on the land as well. It was a clearing ceremony and the settling of protected boundaries. Together we did a part of Barbara-Jean's Four Winds Society Tradition works with stones. We used ritually prepared crystals to secure the property's boundaries and cast a web of security to create a dome of barriers and protection. She taught me how to continue to strengthen and refresh the protection enclosed within. I finally felt empowered and confident that I could perform these tasks. I was finally relieved that I was learning to stay in the light energy. The specifics of exactly all that Barbara-Jean did with me safely standing aside to witness are held securely and privately between my family and us. This is dangerous work, and no one should attempt these ceremonial cleansings without training and protection from a Four Winds Shaman. You can reference this at www.thefourwindssociety.org.

It was such an experience. When she left, I had never heard pure silence in my home before. I could hear my cat's paws walking. It was so silent and peaceful. It felt lighter, and I took the best naps I had ever had in my life. She cleared my home so that I could heal peacefully without disturbance. Two weeks later, Barbara-Jean attended my son's and ex-husband's dual Baptism ceremony. Barbara-Jean, knowing that my ex-husband was not as spiritually awake as I am, approached him to have a conversation thanking him for his cooperation about the home blessing. She asked him how he felt about the home; has it changed? Does he feel more at ease? Has it changed for the better? He confirmed that it was and was thankful for her help.

We didn't stop there. It was only then that I realized I needed to learn how to be consistent and protect my energy, Home, and those I loved as well. I also wanted to clear my energy so that my body was in a truly accepting space to receive healing treatments from the Neurofeedback, psychology work to heal my PTSD, working with physical therapists for my neck, shoulder, arm, left pointer finger, left hip, and lower back. I was willing to do the work to get the maximum healing, and from the brief description I've given about my spiritual experiences, you can see that I was already in an open frame of mind to step outside the box. My Shaman Barbara-Jean had to meet with me having many, many, many sessions, much like therapy sessions with my neuropsychologist and psychologist. We had a total of 37 healing sessions to date. I'd like to remind you that I attended 45 Neurofeedback sessions in one and a half years and 37 healing sessions over a span of eight and a half years with Barbara-Jean. The point being made is that I spent serious amounts of time devoted to all aspects of healing the mind, body, and soul. The topic was just a little different because I was healing past wounds and clearing them from my energy field one by one.

People ask me all the time what a session looks like. It's a lot of work on my friend's part, and I know this after I studied Reiki healing, which I will soon discuss. A lot is done to create a Sacred Space to heal before you ever get to her house. She also needs to keep her own energy in a high vibration in order to be able to complete these sessions and protect herself. Barbara-Jean is above and beyond dedicated to this Shaman life, and I am so grateful she saved me. All sessions begin with an invitation for spiritual help and Archetypes and require a chamber of sacred space to be created by the Shaman. At a session's start that involves healing work, we talk and hone in on a theme. Barbara-Jean is a Master tracker.

I would discuss very deep private fears and things that have happened in the past to me. We would find a linking pattern and then do the work needed to clear it. She tracks the time of the original wounding to clear the trauma. What does that look like? She has spiritually prepared Kuya stones laid out in a beautiful mesa which means table in Spanish but also refers to the flat top mountain. There Kuya stones were hand-picked and ritually prepared to absorb heavy energy in a healing session. They are in a specific pattern. You close your eyes and move your hand around them, stopping at the stone that calls out to you. I feel a vibration, see color and feel the warmth. I then sit across the table from her while she takes notes about the reason that I am there that day. It's usually something that comes up for a specific period of time, for weeks even, that I recognize now needs to be cleared from me emotionally, physically, and spiritually. We talk about it, and she gives her guidance and what she picks up energetically to speak about. I blow all of this into the stone as I am speaking. If I'm angry, I blow it into the stone with everything I got. If I'm crying, I blow that into the stone, giving it everything I've got. My goal is to have this negative energy absorbed into the Kuya stone in order to set it free. I'm using this selected Kuya stone, charging it with my breath, empowered by my intuition to shed the discomforting and disruptive energy. As Baraba-Jean explains, when violence occurs and it is not resolved, it becomes trauma, for a quantum of the life energy flees out of the body that is filled with the trauma energy. The healing sessions involve extracting that disturbed energy and re-installing the original divine quantum of energy that fled.

She uses a test to identify what type of energy is going to be cleared. Then we move to the massage table to be prepared for the clearing. She also holds my head in still point, which not everyone does, but she is trained. I've described this therapy in my healing session with my massage therapist and Osteopath in the previous chapter. She had a similar history, and we shared this injury, so having her heal me was also a gift in itself. Barbara-Jean and I had already done the work acquiring first who the power animal was so we could work with it and care for it back. Conversing spiritually with honor, love, and care. Since we tracked this powerful animal, it is coming to offer service in healing. Here on her property, she has relationships with many animals directly tied to specific clients. Every single time and I mean every single time I leave her home, I have magical events with nature. I have hawks, bald eagles, owls, deer, and such swooping directly around me whether I'm in the car or outside. I literally had this giant buck just casually stand there in front of me, staring at me. He locked eyes with me and then just turned and walked away. I was in awe. I've even had several blue herons fly over my kayak when I was in the years of being able to do that. Her healing sessions are magical, and I don't just go there for healing.

Barbara receives spiritual messages that she needs to share with me and then bestows gifts back into my energy. That was if it was a fairly peaceful reason for being there that day. If I had a particularly serious issue to clear, which had an attachment, she would switch to a completely different mode with me setting to clear it out of my energy with a large ritually prepared crystal for clearing. This is called an extraction, where the goal is to have the Shaman get that energy into the crystal. She would immediately cover it in the mesa until she could clear it. There is a lot of work that has to be done to clear that energy safely out of that crystal. I go there for gatherings during the four big solar holidays. The nature of the work that the Shaman offers training with The Four Winds Society is confidential. The sessions cannot be clearly shared, or the particulars of a session so much are purposefully omitted. I also see her frequently just to hang out because she is an amazing soul. I even go to help her when she needs help. The day she asked me to give her a Reiki healing session just filled my heart with such joy. It was an honor to give that love and to heal the energy back to her that she gave to me. She is one of the most amazing women to heal me. My journey certainly doesn't stop here. She is a lifelong friend of mine now. Recently in a clearing session in January 2023, she gave me information about waiting for a specific person to place a ring lovingly on my hand, symbolizing incoming love. Not on the marriage hand, and as she was giving specific details, I started crying, holding back tears to focus, which in turn made her tear up as well. This is not a normal reaction during one of my sessions with her, and I've been working with her for almost 9 years now. I pointed to the copy of the book that I dropped off to her to pre-read and said, "When you read about what I wrote about not picking a new ring for myself," and showed my hands. I usually have a few rings on, but I had just written about the trauma with my rings and how I felt like no one really knew who I was attached to the rings saying, "The next person who knows me will know what to put on my hand". We are close friends, and she in no way knew that I had written about that, and we never discussed my rings. I'm not even sure she noticed that I was only wearing my "Angel_Tchr" word ring because it is part of my healing work.

At this time, I was also learning Reiki healing because I knew that all avenues of healing must be investigated. I decided to begin Reiki to heal myself because I knew internally that there just had to be more than what this actual world was offering me to heal the best way possible. I just knew, "this is not the end for me" ...try harder, Keli! I was also dealing with a gifted dying mother who was terrified. I was scared and hurting, too, but it was my turn to be the parent and lead her with a fully open heart. I used Reiki to heal her pains and help her with the idea of transitioning to death. I wasn't just fighting for myself, I was fighting indefatigably for both of us. It's easier for me to continue when I can think of someone else and put their needs ahead of mine. It's not easy for me to be alone and just do it for myself. For some reason, it just loses its value, and that sounds ridiculous, but that's where the mind goes during trauma.

I finally got well enough to be able to offer help to my parents, and it was towards the ending time of their lives. My Mother was the person I spoke to multiple times every day for at least 6 years, always encouraging me never to give up. She was afraid of death, and I came close to it, so I, too, was a little nervous about the afterlife. All of the therapies that I was going through to rehabilitate, she was going through as well. She wasn't responding to it as well as I was. I had to remind her many times that healing doesn't always feel good. Often it's very painful, and then with much effort and endurance, you can get to the place where you are no longer in pain. So we were in constant communication cheerleading each other on while yelling at each other when needed out of love and support.

While I was training in Reiki, I was training her. Everything I learned, I would turn and teach her. I had an amazing Reiki Master named Lorry Salluzzi. She was voted "Best Reiki Practitioner" in 2021 & 2022. She trained my massage therapist in Reiki healing years ago. I was so happy to learn of this because I trust this circle of healers very much, so much so that I am sharing my experience, hoping that others take multiple avenues of healing as well. These are people that I am attaching my name to offering truthful relevant healing experiences. I had healing sessions with Lorry, and she is, in fact, the real deal. She is also magical and still practices as well. She is a Reiki Master, Psychic Tarot Reader, and Medium. I truly love her as well as we have stayed in contact over the years. She, too, is just such a positive, loving soul. It's always a pleasure to speak with her. She told me during a healing session (while I was also beginning my Reiki training with her) that I was going to write a book. I laughed and told her she was the second person to say this to me, but I didn't believe her at the time. I knew I was in no place to be able to carry out such a huge project at that time. She was the one who taught me how to understand my "colors" that I see while I am healing others and what it means. I know now how certain colors relate to chakras, but mine also change for healers. There is a very distinct fuschia/bright indigo color that I have described when true healers place their hands on me. It's only now, almost nine years later, that I am able to see a picture of something in weird swirly energy while meditating, often wondering what the heck that was until something happens that day, and then I laugh, understanding why I was shown that vision. I used to be silent about this. Working with Lorry helped me to conduct a Reiki healing session on myself during meditations each morning. At the time surrounding the accident, I did this in the morning and the evening. I have a career in teaching and absolutely love what I do. I admit that I started this Reiki healing journey to help myself and my mother. I couldn't help but feel the pull to help others, but I just didn't have enough confidence in my abilities. I have only put my healing hands on about 10 people. Many of them were in a heightened state and needed immediate help, and it was effective. It gave me confidence that maybe I truly am the healer that I know myself to be. Yes, you'd have to read that back again a second time. I wrote that sentence exactly how it felt, so take it as you will. I do want to heal more people. I just am not in the capacity to travel around, especially because I have a teaching career that is quite busy, and I drive two hours a day to teach. I do appreciate helping friends/family when I can, and I asked them to provide feedback because I wanted to know if I truly had healing hands. Here's what was said in regard to sessions with me: "I suffer from anxiety, and these sessions helped me to relax and feel rejuvenated". Another person shared, "It was a healing, transformative experience; I definitely felt like I had a mind and body reset". Another testimonial is: It was a beautiful experience, it completely turned my day around. Re-energized and was feeling at peace". I have done over-the-phone healing, but I prefer to do healing sessions in person. Recently I again went to my friend's home to help heal the headaches that she was having. It was the first time I had incorporated more of the Shamanism I studied along with Reiki, and it sure proved to be effective. Each time I needed to know an area was healed, I would see a bright white spark of light flash in my mind. When I was holding her head in still point, I started to get this sensation of free falling like I was on a swing, and my friend felt it, too, when I said something out loud. I couldn't help it the healing energy was intense. She helped me with something to do with this book, so I healed her. Energy reciprocity is what healing is all about. Lorry is so amazing she will even (and has offered, but I haven't done it yet but would love to) drop back into classes and review and join healing sessions to keep up with the healing energy work.

It's truly an honor to be introducing my talented healer friends to you all, so you have an idea of where to go for answers when you think there is nowhere else to turn for healing. The work is never done. Never give up. With that said, I would like to tell you all about my friend Tracy Fluty, a Psychic Medium who is part of Elemental Mediums in Upstate New York. Her mission statement, taken directly from her website, is: "Providing Clients and Corporations with spiritual enlightenment through the art and science of Clairvoyance & to encourage the exploration of the indigenous practices of various Holistic Healers for mind, body and spiritual wellness." Tracy is just such an amazing soul. I have shared unique experiences with her that will forever make her a part of my family, quite literally. Tracy has had two articles published in the Saratogian Newspaper. One of the articles was written by her, and one of them was written about her. I found Tracy in such a unique manner. I should really say that the Universe had a beautiful entrance for Tracy to become part of us, meaning me, my sister, and my Mother when she was alive. My sister was given the gift of a healing session with Tracy for one hour in the year 2014. It was actually in June 2014. During this session, our Grandmother came through and gave the date 6/7 a few times. My sister didn't know what that meant but later discovered that was the date of my car accident. There was so much more shared at that session that opened my eyes to what truly is out there for me to learn and understand. I knew I could benefit from speaking to her as well. I called Tracy over the phone for the first time ever in October 2014, four months after my accident. This was when things were getting really heavy in my world with the Traumatic Brain Injury showing itself, going to Neurofeedback treatments, and dealing with the PTSD of the "tailing" from whoever, wherever, whenever (I've discussed this in detail in the PTSD trauma section. Tracy picked up on it right away. The most important piece she ever gave me in that one phone call was my grandmother again coming through saying, "don't even stop the energy work". I could gather what she probably meant at the time but had no idea what it truly meant until now, almost nine years later. She went on to give Tracy validating events, dates, times, and things she could never have known. She also described to me about holding an orange cat. I thought it was Garfield because I was absolutely in love with that character growing up. I later found, while decluttering in the office, a picture of Grandma holding a Garfield in her right hand and a teddy bear in her left hand. I still have that picture that I hold very dear to my heart, which I found in 2014. What's even crazier is that in 2019 I got my parents an orange cat at their request since they were devastated over the loss of their fur baby named Cali. My Mom was then put in a nursing home, and this orange cat named Simba was the only comfort to Dad. This information shared with me not only provides validation that it was indeed Grandma chatting from the other side but a glimpse of recognizing the future path.

It didn't stop here for the relationship with Tracy. Of course, I set up another session to see her bringing my sister with me. Initially, it was because, during this time, my brain injury was at its worst, and she came along to help me remember what Tracy was going to tell me. During this time, my cell phone, my Mom, and my sister were my lifelines to remembering whatever I needed to know. On the way to get to Tracy's office, I stopped at Barnes & Noble, and I swear to you, this book came flying off the shelf in front of my face and fell to the ground. It was about becoming a writer. I picked it up and put it back, thinking there was no way that was an accident but not really understanding what just happened. I took a picture of it to show my sister to explain what happened and see what she thought of it. Like I've been saying this whole book, my guides are very strong. When we got to the session with Tracy, she immediately told me, "You know, you write a book about all of this healing you're doing". I laughed and said, "I don't see that happening". She was so sure of it that she even shared a class to take in the Adirondacks on how to start writing your own book. I signed up for the class and never went. That wasn't the last time a healer told me I would write a book. Of course, I brought my Mother and sister to her in a group session another day. She was able to speak about direct relatives of my Mother that my sister and I had no information on whatsoever. We didn't even know the names spoken or how they were related to us, but Mom knew exactly what was happening. My favorite part of this session was Tracy yelling out in a confused voice, "Walk the puppy"! Why am I hearing someone laughing and yelling, "walk the puppy". We all laughed so hard because it was our code to take Dad out of the house somewhere. He would get so anxious to go somewhere and do something, and I came up with the phrase when I called my Mom, saying, "Okay, I'm going to come to walk the puppy". I created this phrase as code originally because if my Dad knew I was coming to take him out, I would receive about 15 calls asking "if I'm there yet" because I live an hour away, and he would get so excited. He did it to all of us kids;

actually, he truly enjoyed the most mundane trips out into the world. These are things that people don't just know. Tracy is absolutely in touch with relatives and such on the other side, and it's so beautiful. Not only did she meet my mother in the here-and now-world, but she is also able to tell me things while Mom is on the other side. My mother communicates with me in many ways as well. She uses instances with my cats all the time to send messages or make me focus on certain things. She'll have them knock things over that I need to pay attention to. As I'm typing this, my female cat (she loves calico cats) is dancing around my feet, meowing for no other reason than to just say hello. Calire doesn't usually do this and certainly has not in either of the homes we have lived in.

My Dad, on the other hand, is quite hilarious and plays pranks. I'm going to weave in a personal snippet of how Dad interacts with me from the other side. I have to digress from Tracy for a moment just to prove that this does actually happen to me quite often. Mom and Dad were both dying from diabetes. They hid candy or anything we would try to throw out on them all over the house when we came over, which was basically all the time between the three of us. We found all of this after they passed and were appalled. I mean marshmallows, candy bars, you name it, hidden in every crevice. I was laughing and thinking, "Oh my God, I think they forgot about half of this that they hid". Two days after

Dad's death, I woke up alone in the house and went to the kitchen for coffee. I found marshmallows thrown all over the kitchen floor. The bad was hanging from a hidden cabinet above the microwave. I didn't know these were there at all. My ex-husband placed them up there to stop our son from eating the whole bag. I called him at work to see if he saw this before he left, and he said no. I shared pictures but laughed hysterically. This was proof that he was with me the whole time while clearing his home. In true Jack form, he showed me that he is still here with us. So hearing this describes his character. On the spiritual side, he'll talk away to anyone he thinks can also channel him to get messages to me. He is always with Tracy and me when we get together. She says he cracks her up, and that makes total sense. He never held back and loved to be an entertainer and the center of attention. Tracy is just so funny too. One time I went to an event in Saratoga to see her. It was a packed banquet room, and I went with my sister and some of her friends. I was really hoping to have her friends get their names pulled so that they could go up and meet with Tracy. They had something going on for themselves, and the caretaker in me really wanted to help and get her answers for my sister. When he got our numbers, I turned to my sisters' friends and said, "If my number is pulled, I will give it to you". I already met with Tracy often, and we even chatted in short texts here or there, so I knew I would be working with her again for sure. I wanted to help my sisters' friends. The first thing Tracy did was introduce herself and say, "Just so you know if your number was called, don't think you're going to pass it off and give it to someone else. Spirit has chosen you, and you are the one that needs to come up here". I started laughing. Then I was the second person called, and I started laughing again. Tracy and I just keep getting aligned. Recently I went to see her in June and then again in November 2022. I love my healers and friends so much that I can barely contain the love that I have for these gifted healers as I write about them. I exchange texts with her as well. She is determined to help me with such a loving heart. We have worked together so long that all gloves are off when I go to visit. Often there is ridiculous laughter, tears, and back and forth because we have genuinely formed a bond, and Tracy wants to guide me to the best possible feeling for everything I have been through. Very much like my visits with my psychologist and Shaman, she definitely tells me to get focused. She shoves me a little in the right direction when I get a little sad or off track. I adore her to the moon and back. I am so truly blessed that she was sent to be a part of my healing soul tribe.

During this same time of healing with Barbara-Jean, Lorry, and Tracy, I was also working with a friend named Karen Roberts, who is a magnificent healer as well. Taken directly from her website: "Karen is a Divine Communicator and author who credits her Divine Guidance for bringing healing miracles to Earth through her. After a profound spiritual awakening in 2008, Karen was guided toward her life purpose as an Energy Healer. After completing, graduating, and becoming certified in Shamanism, Angel Therapy, and Golden Atlantis, Karen's perceptive healing talents have evolved to an original combination of what she has learned and her ability to listen to God and the Light Beings who work through her." Like Karen, I am taking everything that I have learned through my Shamanic sessions/training and Reiki, along with my own personal studies of Angels, which I will talk about after the viewpoint of my positive healing experiences with Karen. I, too, have intertwined what I have studied and made healing sessions using parts of everything that I have learned. Karen wrote a book titled While You Were Dreaming. The description is also taken directly from her book website Karenroberts.com/book: "While You Were Dreaming is a compilation of my own spiritual journey accompanied by divine channels that come to me in the middle of the night. These channels come from my Divine guidance and were spoken to me by the light beings associated with Ascended Master Saint Germain. They are meant to be shared with the world, and they will apply directly to your life. Everything about this book is healing, from the cover to the words, to the intention behind it, to the effect that it may have in your life." It was the first Shaman that I ever met, who introduced me to my loving Shaman friend Barbara-Jean that led me to Karen. We were both studying angels at the time. She had mentioned a positive healing session with Karen and encouraged me to give this a chance as well. Knowing that I was a completely open, spiritually gifted person in search of true healers, I agreed to have a session and did so in the year 2014. I have had at least two sessions a year since then with Karen. My guides often let me know when it's time to call her healing services. I am in contact with her, however, since we have had many sessions and have grown quite fond of friendship. It's easy to adore these women. They are true love and light. Karen calls via Facetime and video chat and speaks to you for the first 30 minutes, channeling information that needs to get to you. She was able to even tell me things about my home, the energy, and my son, who was in a completely different part of the home at the time. She even helped me with things to do with my cats at that time. The things she knew/knows from divine communication with Angels are just amazing. She was also able to tell me that I was going to write a book. She even gave me warnings about the process of it and such. So that makes four people that were telling me that I was going to write a book. I kept telling them that they were wrong, yet here I am, almost nine years later, telling my story to help others heal conventionally but also to heal spiritually and step outside of the box. She knew that I was not supposed to remain in that home and gently shared with me that I would be leaving that home at some point. I was horrified at this and thought, well, I was trying to move due to my PTSD. I had to drive that curve where I was hit multiple times a day, and I just wanted to get away from it, so I was searching for a new home but then stopped. I decided to just focus on my healing and remain where I was. Selling wasn't beneficial at that time either, so it wouldn't have worked out in the years 2014-2016 anyways, for many reasons. It just wasn't the time, but she knew I wasn't staying there. She also gently tried to get me to address my marriage at a time when I had no energy for the fight. It wasn't going well, but I was fighting to heal to get back to teaching and regain my life. I was busy being a Mom to a seven-year-old son. I was busy saving my parents. I was just always too busy to address how much I was carrying alone. She knew because the day I called for a session, the first thing she did was talk about the decision I had made. It was an extremely difficult session with ridiculous amounts of crying because it felt like a failure, but it just wasn't going to work. She offered guidance and healed me. Karen speaks with you channeling the first half, and then heals you for the second portion. I go all out, I lay down, and I close my eyes, and I treat it the same way I would treat all of my healing sessions. I always feel whenever she is healing. She finds it so entertaining to work as a healer because I can tell her exactly what she is focusing on because I feel the energy vibration. It's like a tingling, like a part of you being asleep and coming back to normal blood flow. Sometimes I'll also hear something or see an image in my head, and we talk about it and giggle. I'm definitely my strongest when working in a pair with someone who is a healer or also spiritually gifted. I cherish Karen and her healing abilities. She has changed my life for the better in so many ways. She and I also will get into that "no sugar coating, I know what's best for you" family type of healing. It's done out of soul tribe love, and I truly adore her. Like Tracy, she had healing sessions with my Mom via Facetime before entering the nursing home and provided in-detail information very relevant to what was needed to be healed. She was also the last healer to Facetime her while she was in Home Hospice a few days before she passed, giving her comforting information to ease her fears. It's so humbling and wonderful to know these women spoke to my Mother and are still guiding me to the best place in life that I can possibly be.

While I was in my room in pain, trying desperately to heal, I was studying Angels. I was following a woman named Doreen Virtue. She had a call in a radio show, and she was living in Hawaii at the time. Doreen was a spiritual teacher and therapist and taught Angel Therapy courses. Angel Therapy is a type of alternative therapy that includes working with archangels and guardian angels to heal different health issues, including mental, physical, and spiritual problems. Naturally, this was someone I looked up to while going back to church, studying angels, and healing. I called the radio show and got picked to speak to her three different times. My Shaman friend was amazed because it was impossible to get through. I did, and on both occasions, she told me, "You have very loud angels". I laughed and was not surprised by this information. I know my ancestors, and I always knew I had some divine link and was protected on the other side. I knew this from a very young age. I literally lived my life like God was watching me all the time. I thought it was odd, but it kept me right where I needed to be and protected. I couldn't understand why I was in this accident. This conversation I had with her literally had me wondering how directly tied all of my healers were. I had just come from my massage therapist and was feeling pretty glum. I shared with Dianne, my massage therapist, that I was angry and wanted my life back. This was the point of healing that massages were for medical purposes only, and I really had to ramp myself up to go. It was difficult healing work. It was not glamorous and quite often would keep me in pain for the day, all for the sake of getting back movement and undoing damage to my structure and muscles. Dianne, my trusted massage therapist, told me that I was like a cake being baked in the oven, and it was time for me to come out yet. I still had baking that needed to be done at a certain temperature and a certain amount of time, or the cake would not come out right. I listened and huffed and went home to make this call to Doreen. She told me the exact same story almost verbatim, and I was in total shock. She used the same analogy to guide me to continue with my healing efforts. I was lucky enough to get through to her twice. I have a blue stone that was hers that I purchased off of eBay, and I wear it when I am called to do so. I read her Mary Queen of Angels book and just loved it as I called on her often. I also have her Mary Queen of Angel Oracle Cards. I read almost everything Doreen has written, including Don't Let Anything Dull Your Sparkle. She was a brief study for a period of time that left me with things that I would intertwine with my future healing studies. I still have her Angel Numbers reference book as well. I have now moved on to studying the works and teachings of Kyle Gray. I enrolled in his Angel Team courses which, admittingly, I need to complete, and it's been quite a few months. Sorry, Kyle, I got distracted writing my book (insert giggling).

Chapter 6

Now I'm going to enlighten everyone about the exact circumstances which led me to become close friends with Patti Negri, who is a famous Hollywood Psychic Medium endearingly called The Good Witch. She always teaches positive self-talk, focusing on the mind, body, and spirit in her classes. She has a podcast series called The Witching Hour. A few of her guests I've had the pleasure of meeting, and they are just lovely individuals. I've been asked about this so many times it's about time it's in print so everyone will hear the absolute truth about how we came to be friends. I need you to step back into my timeline that I have already shared and remember that I have been through the following traumas in succession: hit by a drunk driver and had a brain injury with other ailments requiring years of rehabilitation; healing PTSD and triggers; helping my parents while they were in their phase of dying at the same time; teaching during a pandemic (which I will speak of in following chapter); home hospice care for Mother while Dad had an accident and died first leaving us instant orphans; and then divorce. Something happened during the month of November 2020. It was nighttime and five months after the death of my parents. I was sitting in the hot tub, and I had a firm hand holding my left shoulder from behind. It wasn't a malicious feeling but was a solid "I'm here" type of acknowledgment. I turned around, expecting to see my ex-husband or my son, and there was nothing. I stood straight up, running into the house, leaving all the hot tub jets running and the lid open. I told my ex-husband exactly what happened, and you'd think he would just understand my story and how I had a gift. He did not and was not happy about having to go outside and close everything up while I ran away. Our marriage wasn't good, and this wasn't greeted well. I got no comfort or support, and it truly rattled me to the core of my heart. It was then, finally, after all the talks with my psychologists, healers, and this happening, that I realized it was time to move on from this marriage. He, too, was also demonstrating it was time to move on, and it was mutually agreed upon action.

I always watched paranormal shows (obviously, if you've read this book, you certainly get why I do). I wasn't seeking a thrill from anything. I lived my life in fear of my gift, and I watch these shows to gather strength and learn how to live and protect myself. Included in the shows I have always followed were Ghost Adventures. Yep, that included the good-looking Zachary Bagans. I'm starting to giggle as I type this because two years later, I understand what my spirit team was doing. At the time, however, I was just "in it to win it, I guess". They had to find a way to make me pay attention to a highly specific spiritual path, and Zak was the way they got me to pay attention. Easy to do while watching him, still smirking. Just like a million other ladies, yes, he is easy to look at with the eyes. But there was something that happened that changed me. No, we were not going to fall in love and get married. I had a dream that night that I was grabbed in the hot tub. That night in my sleep, I can still recall this dream two years plus later, I was being consoled about my fear from the hot tub incident. I remember being hugged firmly, and I backed into the cuddle to enjoy the protection and comfort. When I turned around, I didn't see my ex-husband, I saw Zak. I shared this dream with my sister, and of course, in true sister fashion, this set off a frenzy of Zak Bagans photos and such, including Valentine's day gift with his photo on it. My son painted a wooden circle stating "I love Zak Bagans" to give to me. Stay with me, and I'll explain this in detail, and it definitely leads me, through Zak's work, to Patti, which was where the spirit was trying to bring me. I just want to relive a few of the dynamics from studying Zak as closely as I did. I watched everything he made. I read his books. I'm not a fan, girl. I don't follow people because they are just hunky or famous, that's not how I operate. I will, however, admit that I am able to fixate on someone that I am trying to learn from. Zak was taking a journey that not many would understand in his own personal endeavors. He battles his own fears and still rises to the occasion while holding personal things and anxiety to the side. Spiritually he represented the path I needed to take to gain back control of the "unseen" portion of my life that I still wasn't comfortable sharing everywhere, even at the age of 43. That dream I had where Zak was holding me meant something other than just physical attention. It meant spiritual protection. My sister was actually the one who pointed out to me that the dream represented an idea of a person who would understand me and the life that I lead. That made total sense to me, but I couldn't help but be over-captivated.

Through this experience and search for knowledge, I noticed Patti Negri on a few of his shows. I randomly looked her up and saw that she and her bestie, Merle Singer (co-leader with Patti the Relationship and Miracle Worker), author of the book cracking the Relationship Code, were running a relationship course. I was thinking, are we serious? Of course, I need this help! I took the course and still to this day follow up once a month. I'm not paired up with my ideal match yet, but they were absolutely there for me in every way during my divorce. I got separated in January 2021, with him moving out immediately with a completed mutual divorce in June 2021. I did not request this. He was already planning to leave, and this was just the final catalyst. He literally packed one Wednesday and left that Friday for good in January. I started this course with Patti and Merle after the separation happened. Their course was supposed to focus on how to move forward and find a match. For me, however, this was a complicated task. They had to get me to a place where I loved myself again. They had to get me to accept a compliment without trying to brush it away. They taught me how to learn to accept a gift of kindness. I don't have to be so strong all the time, which is survivor mode. I was learning how to move from survivor mode to just being myself. We had many classes, emails, and then texts to help me improve my life. I won't even get into the specifics of what they taught me in totality because the point of this is to demonstrate the intense friendship connection. It was so strong that I decided to fly out to Vegas to meet her. I had a friend that I brought along to enhance her spiritual growth as well, who was also in the class with me. There are two females that I met in this class that I am still speaking with closely, and it's 2023. I am flying out to see them in February 2023. In Vegas, at an event, I met my wonderful friend Alicia Gutierrez and her husband, Ramon. Alicia is an Astrologist and Psychic Medium who works under the name Cosmic Divine. We instantly became friends, and she placed a moldavite ring on my finger that was very dear to her. We joke all the time because she placed it on my wedding finger and said, "I see Angel wings on you," before even hearing what I was really about. She was the inspiration for the clothes I wore in one of my first photoshoots. She is extremely talented in communicating, and I can offer countless times she knew things that just truly had never been discussed. She is very rooted and spiritually guided, and guarded. Jumping ahead, I have also befriended Kristi Grissom from Our Haunted Lives. She, David, Patti, and I had some absolute laughs at this last event in MA in October 2023. Kristi and I talk in hanging out sessions that are just truly healing to the soul mixed in with wild times. We jokingly refer to how I am the random Earth Angel that drops in, and it's all perfectly normal to be around each other. I am that energy that can work around any type of energy due to everything I have been through, plus my studies and line of work.

Getting back to the topic of my Vegas trip in June of the year 2021, we excitedly went to Zak's museum, and that day; me, Patti, my friend Victoria, and Patti's bestie Sebastian had a visit during the tail end of the pandemic. I've always been intrigued yet terrified to visit this museum, and it certainly lives up to its reputation, so please go in there protected and clear. I had a blast knowing that I could see such a place while being highly spiritually protected by two powerful people. I'll never forget crawling through the pitch-black tunnel with Patti behind me, and all of a sudden, I feel my pants come undone at the legs. I laughed and yelled, "Patti, you undid my pants! She yells out, "I can't see in here it's dark". She has the same exact playful heart and light energy that I do. I literally feel like she is a family member of mine, a true soul tribe member. Throughout the museum, as I experienced things, all I did was motion to her, and she would guide me. She already knew what I was sensing. Her constant feedback is not to hold onto it or fight back. Just release it. Breathe! She feels this pull, too, kindred spirit-wise, soul tribe adoration, as we have discussed. She calls it a "soul pod". This is where my true growth really skyrocketed while she helped me to see that I was a beautiful person. I felt worn out, abandoned, and just lost, and Patti made sure that I understood just how blessed I was. She actually refers to me as an Earth Angel. She'll very casually tell you, "oh yeah, Keli's an Earth Angel".

I drove to Salem, MA, to see Patti in April 2021 before flying to Vegas in June 2021. My sister, who was now the matriarch of the family, wanted to make sure that my multiple traumas weren't sending me over the edge, so to speak. She was nervous as she did not come close to the spiritual encounters that I have had in my life. This was a little too outside the box for her, but she wanted to make sure that she saw it with her own eyes that these people were good people and safe. Their words and encounters with us were nothing short of miraculous, where my sister was so impressed. I could tell that she was totally relieved for more than one reason. These friends were safe, and I could finally find a place where I was no longer alone. This was comforting to someone who is worried about their sister after losing everything. I had my career, which I absolutely love. I love humans and adore interacting with everyone. I am a social chameleon in the best way. My son has kept me fighting to be the best version I can possibly present because I want him to see what one can overcome. He has shared with me that he wants to be a psychologist, and that makes my heart dance. It was Tracy who told me years ago, right after the accident, "your son will be a healer because of what you show him".

I drove to see Patti in Salem again when it was her birthday. I text her and speak to her online. I took/take when my schedule opens, several classes online with her and the University Magickus. It taught me how to take charge and protect myself against unseen things that were constantly trying to get my attention. It included studying with a few of her colleagues, which really opened my eyes to the other side. I am grateful for all the knowledge that I have acquired in the past 8 years of spiritual studies.

I drove out to spend time with her recently in Concord, MA, and of course, every encounter with her brings more joy and laughter each time now that we lovingly know things about each other. We have no problems passing jokes with and at each other, and it's just so much fun. I am flying out to see her again in California as well as my friends Merle and Cristina Terzes. Cristina is the beautiful, talented artist friend who painted the rising Phoenix art piece in many of my social media posts. She also has her own brand of accessories that she creates and just has pure talent and a wonderfully supportive and loving soul. I'm very excited to see her in her own home atmosphere in LA. Each time I see her, it is more magical than the last time. She is aware of me writing this book and knows I am mentioning her as a significant healing part of my life. She is just such a beautiful white light energy that has a wonderful way of telling you without sugarcoating what's needed to be done to enhance your life. She's full of laughter and smiles, and I'm just so happy that the world of Zak Bagans led me to her and her healing capacities.

Chapter 7

Teaching during the pandemic is the catalyst of change that set my future aflame like wildfire. While trying to balance the traumas and heal, the inside of our very large school building started showing signs of an impending illness. Collectively we had all been in and out of the building with varying symptoms. I'm a Kindergarten Reading Specialist, so I am no stranger to coughing, sneezing, etc., in close proximity while they're still learning how to cover their noses and such. We think nothing of it as it's part of the job in these lower grades to "learn routine" and "manners". It's an absolute pleasure always working with them. There's never a dull moment with their words and characters making my heart dance inside. With that said, classroom attendance was starting to dwindle. The news stations were reporting this Global Pandemic COVID.

During this time, both of my parents were in need of serious help. My father had collapsed, hitting his head (this was the first time he had hit his head in a fall resulting in a brain injury also). At that particular fall (he was always collapsing because he did his best but didn't have the money and was, unbeknownst to me, rationing his insulin for his diabetes. That's a long tragic story in itself, and a few of my earlier Instagram video posts explain this in detail about the absolute injustice of a simple med to keep people with

Diabetes alive. Insurance doesn't cover all of it, and then the bill is over $400 a month additionally to stay alive. Quite often, I paid out of my own pocket for his meds when he told me. He even got some free insulin pens from the doctors because they, too, were worried that the system was unfair.

I hadn't heard from Dad, and this was not usual, so we started checking around to find out he had been taken to the hospital. He managed to crawl to the phone to call for help. He didn't even use the safety alert bracelet that I made him keep on paying monthly so I could "ping him", and I'm laughing because that's how much I cared. I actually called the company and pinged his location when I was worried. I was pacing frantically in my home back and forth, back and forth, with my son watching me. He was on edge because he knew this was not a normal action I was doing, and he could feel something wrong. When I received the call that he had hit his head and broken multiple parts of his ribs, with some ribs being broken in several parts alone, I let out a scream that shook my ancestors. This man had suffered so much. They described that this was going to be a painful healing process, that he would be there for a while, and that I would not be able to visit him because they were locked down. I was beside myself emotionally. I had Dad in the hospital, and I had Mom in a nursing home, and my siblings and I got locked out of seeing them. We had no warning and were not prepared. They had no tablets, and their cell phones worked when they remembered how to use them or even heard them ringing in the first place. This is the emotional state I was in before the life-altering news was delivered in regard to our teaching careers.

In March 2020, it was a Thursday, and I was in my classroom checking on my father, who was brought to Albany Medical Hospital. It was sent in email form to take all belongings home, and this was our move to teaching virtually only. Standing there in shock as I looked around the room, grabbing pieces that I think will be the most important. It wasn't just leaving the building; we were not allowed to enter back into it. I took a good ¼ of my classroom because, at this pivoting point, I still had not yet mastered the art of teaching virtually. We were given every single training known available to quickly use. I signed up for so many classes that I feel like I earned an extra Master's degree in Technology without the actual credit for doing so. Every single one of us was doing this at the same time all over the world. We became a collective group that would spend hours calling, texting, sharing ideas, and just collaborating on mass levels to try to keep these students learning. This was matched by trying to teach parents of five-six-year-olds how to log onto the Chromebooks and get their young child to join on a screen and focus with attention to learn like college students. I'm not even touching the surface of that discussion alone, as we had all now stepped into the uncomfortable part of "seeing into everyone's private lives". It was just as uncomfortable for us collectively; this I know for sure. Now you weren't teaching students either, you were teaching students with parents sitting right there in the sessions as well, which added a whole other level of "stage fright" for a minute until adjusted. My superpower at that time was nonjudgment. And some background in entertainment. I was kind and caring at all times and just made everyone feel that whatever they were doing was good enough.

My position as a Kindergarten Reading Specialist was tricky to figure out because the schedules had to be catered to classroom schedules. Sometimes I would join the main classrooms and attempt to assist students personally, help on the side, and help present something to do with the whole group. After many mishaps and fumbled attempts, it was easier for me to assign smaller group meetings at any other time than the classroom times. I even made special one-to-one sessions because the only thing that mattered was that I logged on and taught.

With both of my parents dying at the same time, in the hospital and nursing home, I was just being pulled in every direction. I would even have to wake up hourly at night and call into the hospital and nursing home for check-ins. Often I would spend five hours a day driving to work, then to Albany, and back down to my area because I had to be at the hospital for my parents. My sister and brother were local and were a constant presence. The three of us were rotating visits, and it just wasn't good enough. We always felt like we just couldn't do enough. There was so much at one time, and we often felt worn out and guilty. I just didn't want to miss the last time I could hear them, God forbid. I was always on edge. After all the healing I did and finally getting to a place where I could balance, my world was literally tossed upside down again.

My Principal Bosses, as I gave a shout-out to earlier, are just an amazingly understanding, talented, and supportive Administration team. At this time, I only had my Principal (Boss, as I call her), Nicole Ey. She was extremely supportive and always guided me to make the best of what I could do. She encouraged me to try my best, and it was going to be enough because it was something. She saw my tears and how hard I was fighting to keep my job while attempting to help my parents, which was a battle. I had another Literacy Support Specialist who I follow, and she had many conversations with me getting to understand what I was going through and then watching me step up to the plate and keep doing my job. Rebecca Maher has a heart of gold, for sure. Shout out to the teams that drove to my house for a car birthday parade. I just can't print enough how wonderful my colleagues are. We fight like family at times and stand behind each other in solidarity when we need to.

Every day I woke up not knowing if that day was the day one of them was going to die. I moved Dad to the same nursing home in hopes that they would be together. Everyone assured me this was a good plan. Dad didn't want to go, but my siblings nor I could take care of him on our own. He needed serious rehabilitation services. Reluctantly I got him there because he spent every single day at my mother's side at that nursing home before his last large fall. I would receive calls that he was bossing nurses around, acting as if he lived there. When I offered for him to live there, he refused. It was a constant fight with the nursing home, from mishaps to Dad's shenanigans to Mom's medical needs.

As soon as he arrived, they kept him away from her because he was in a hospital and needed to isolate him due to COVID procedures. This sent him into a frenzy, and it sent me there also, as I was being assured this was the best option for him. With his head injury, he was moody and just confused most of the time, so this wasn't helping. He was just so emotionally upset that he couldn't just walk down the hall and see his wife of 59 years. My siblings and I took turns driving to the nursing home, visiting the windows to see my parents. I fought hard to finally let me see them at the same time. They had one person at each of their sides. They were in wheelchairs a good four feet apart, and we talked with these people standing guard. I didn't care and acted normally, cracking jokes left and right, and the ladies learned to love these strange window visits. When I drove away, I saw an old man outside his wife's window, and he was sitting on the walker parked by the window. He was hot and tired and was laying his head on the window screen. He was there every day. I cried and still am crying now, recalling this visual because I knew what he was feeling, but I was a lot younger, and this had to be emotionally and physically breaking for him. My parents knew their time was coming. They hated the way of the world at the moment and started asking us to constantly bring their favorite foods. The nursing home was fighting back for a bit until I went all "bulldog," as Mom used to call me. They were dying and knew it. All they wanted to do at this time was do it in style. I signed my father out of the nursing home despite all of my reservations at the end of May 2020. I signed my mother out as outside Home Hospice Care around the same time. My Mom didn't want to pass away in the nursing home. She wanted to come home to pass away, but my Dad was in such denial that he had us bring her to my sister's home, thinking he could somehow stop the dying process with this refusal.

I believe it was my birthday weekend because she was only with us until June 16, 2020. My Dad visited my Mom at my sister's house. June 13, 2020. He said to Mom as she was just lying there, mostly unresponsive at this point, leaning down over her and with all of us there said, "Oh, they're coming Monday? Okay, I'll see you then". I literally yelled out, "What the hell did he just say"? I again yelled to my siblings, "What did he just say"? We were trying to ask him what he had just heard and why he said that, and he was just as lost in his confusion as ever. This is important so stay with me. We had an outside gathering to just get some air and have Dad outside. My brother was walking him around the yard. He wasn't even using his walker and was struggling, and I yelled, "Dad, you're supposed to use the walker, not carry it," and he gave me the middle finger. I laughed out loud as this was something our silly family did to each other. Some of the last pics are of my hand with my Mom's hands. Her fingers were crippled, and her bent middle finger with mine, looking straight at the camera together. We had a very comical loving relationship, so this was a normal response that made me smile for a second.

He left, and we again didn't hear from him that next day at all. Twelve hours of "unaccounted for Jack" meant something was wrong. I called his neighbor across the street named, Paul. He and his family generationally knew us collectively. He had keys to the home of my parents. When he called me, my face said everything in the world to my sister. I didn't say a word and just shook. It was a mass amount of guilt that surged through my body. We had spent 11 days waiting by my mother's side to help her pass away, unafraid, surrounded by people. That's why I pulled her out of the nursing home so we could be by her side in her passing. Instead, my father had another fatal diabetic shock fall, hitting his head. Paul working in Emergency Services with a wonderful reputation, had everyone there and was taking care of it so that none of us would have to witness this. He tried to keep my brother out of the house, but my brother went in and saw my Dad in that state. My sister and I were by Mom's side. I, on the next day, had to meet my brother at the funeral home while my sister was still at my Mom's side.

The woman from the funeral home asked me if I wanted to see him, and I said, "Yes, please. I need to see him"? The woman left but then quickly came back to me with a shocked face and again asked me, "are you sure you want to see him"? I answered yes again. She looked at my brother and said, “Did you see your Dad at the house”? My brother’s eyes welled up, and all he could do was nod his head in agreement, and then I could read the energy. I just gasped in tears thinking, “Oh my God, brother, what did you see”? I know what trauma is and what it feels like to overcome it, so my attention was now on how to help my brother erase the visual. She said, “We’re going to need some time to get him visible”. They didn’t even have room for us to see him in the pretty room. He was in a white hallway, with a white sheet placed over him. That was the last time I ever saw him. We had plans of cremation, so I knew this was it. The process was started. Going back to when he leaned over Mom and said, “Okay, I’ll see you then,”... Dad always had to be first. Mom passed June 16, 2020, only 36 hours after Dad.

While still transitioning Mom to her death, we were on a timer. The only thing that Mom could eat was the tiniest, and I mean smaller than my pinky nail pieces of watermelon. I remember begging her to eat, and her mouth was dry. There was no way she could drink anything and keep it down, and she couldn’t eat; she choked. I went to the grocery store, stood there looking worn and staring blankly at the fruit section. I saw a red watermelon pre-sliced in a container. I thought to myself, that has juice, I can make it small, it will dissolve, and she won’t choke. To this day, whenever I see watermelons, I'm mixed with remembering feeding these to her when she needed them and love at the same time.

When the timer would ring, my sister and I would have to jump up and continue to feed fatal drugs to our mother. I was lying in a lazyboy chair on my left side, facing her in the bed. My sister was in another one set up behind me, sleeping. I was staring at my Mom at 2 AM, and I said, "Dad, where are you? You said you were going to be here, where are you". Then I yelled to my Mom, "It's time to go. Dad's already there. It's time to go. Get out of that body and pinch my butt cheek and go". She always gave me goosies as her little girl. I felt a touch on my cheek that was in the air because I was on my left side. I froze, and I literally watched her body inhale big and then exhale what seemed like forever with no replenishing of air. I stared at her lips and chest so hard I was searching for any sign. Then I went to her body, already knowing as I felt her grab me that she had finally left. I was standing, and my sister caught the energy and flew out of the chair yelling, "Is it time, is it time"? Again, just like the phone call about Dad's death, she saw that same look, and I just shook my head "no," meaning no more drug panics because she had finally passed. Then we sat in silence by her side.

We had a dual memorial service as they were both cremated. They even had Dad in the wrong urn, and I just thought that was so appropriate for the time that I was having. We had their ashes mixed together in glass hearts to keep in our home, which I have posted several pictures of on my social media accounts. Then later got a tattoo of a rising Phoenix in the same blue and green colors as the glass heart on my right forearm. It's to look at for myself to remember everything that I've been through and to remember them. I look down at it. It's facing me because it is meant for me. It's my way of still hearing Mom and Dad say, "go, little bulldog, go".

That first holiday, Thanksgiving 2020, we couldn't be together because family members had COVID. That second holiday we had to do Christmas Eve through Facetime. I did drive up, and we had mimosas on the front lawn in full outdoor attire because it was cold but because we were determined if only for an hour, to see each other. It was the most heartbreaking holiday season I have ever experienced, and that's a lot because, for the past two years, I have been completely alone on Christmas from 9 AM until a few days from then due to my divorce.

Circling back to the Home Hospice Care in itself. You are not prepared to be a full-time nurse by yourself. There are things they don't tell you that can and will happen because of the shock factor. We had three to four people help honor Mom's wishes. Mom was tough and had literally no kidney function at all left and was telling me she wanted to get up. One time she looked at me and said, "I'll never forgive you for this. I'll never forgive you for doing this to me". It was the massive amounts of fatal drugs I was giving her, but it ripped my heart right out of my chest. My sister and her husband were able to isolate it and even pass some jokes because they understood. However, I was recovering from trauma after trauma after trauma, and this was not what I wanted to hear after fighting with everything I had left to save her for as long as I could. I was constantly making split-second decisions for her, which terrified me. Before her first port was ever put in to start dialysis years before, they said that she would not make the surgery. They made me decide in front of my Dad whether to take the chance or not, but she was dying, and this was a time extension. I told them to go ahead with the procedure. My Dad screamed at the doctor and screamed at me because he was frightened and didn't want to take the chance. This was important because, at that very time, her legs were splitting apart and leaking because her body couldn't get rid of the fluids. She was in excruciating pain, so it wasn't just a matter of time, it was humanity. My Dad started crying and turned to me and said, "I hate you, and I don't forgive you". That surgery gave

Mom one more year of life and experience with it. It was the same way when I had to take Mom out of his home and put her in the nursing home. He cried so hard that I was concerned he was going to have a heart attack right then and there. It was sobbing that I can't even describe it just ripped me apart. I still feel the loss that he felt at that time. It wasn't the first time that my Dad had to tell me how angry he was at me, but I was simply the one in charge of making the best decisions out of options that had no pleasant ending at all. I always consulted with my sister but had to pull the trigger and fight with doctors, hospitals, nursing homes, and at some times, lawyers as well. It was a difficult and very solitary stack of pressure.

I knew so many people who had shared the same traumas as me, and I was diligent in going and getting help. But NONE of them walked ALL of these traumas in short succession, toppling on me emotionally. Meanwhile, I still worked and was still a Mom. My friend went through this Home Hospice event with her Mom. We had never spoken in detail about what she went through, but after I walked it, and I had already taken her to see Tracy for a healing session, we talked about what she saw. We were able to share the darkest, and I mean darkest, things that we had to do for our mothers as they were dying that is not shared by Home Hospice when you agree to this. My heart literally bleeds for people, and you can see it in my eyes when I hear the words Home Hospice. It takes special angels to get that job done. I can't emphasize that enough.

I have shared these moments with all of you so that you have someone's inside point of view about the healing journey and what goes on. I want to reiterate that there is no "perfect" healing journey. There are many nights of tears and crying so loud with my face lying flat on the ceramic tile floor. There were days when I would sit in absolute silence, staring out the bedroom window, just praying. The night my Dad died, I drove one hour home, walked in the front door kicking my sandals off, grabbed a full bottle of wine, walked down the back stairs, out the back door, and got directly into the hot tub drinking that bottle of wine sobbing uncontrollably. My son, not knowing what happened, stood above me, confused, like "why does she have her clothes on", but sympathetic, knowing the circle of traumas occurring. He thought Grandma had passed, totally shocked to hear Grandpa died, realizing instantly that his Mom was about to lose both of her parents at once. There is no perfection in grief and how it's handled. The goal is to handle it as safely as you can. Perfection does not exist. I dare you to explain to me what perfection is, and we will spend hours talking until you realize perfection is only a matter of perception. I am not a depressed person, but there were so many traumas toppled onto me at the same time. Every time I beat one trauma, another one would pop up like a never-ending game of whack-a-mole. Healing is not perfect, so do everything you can to take any step forward and heal a tiny bit each day.

Chapter 8

With all of my traumas thrown into the spotlight, hoping to encourage others on the road to recovery or healing somehow, I now want to share some of the most beautiful moments of this self-discovery. There were times that I started shocking people with my next moves working in silence. The first time I shocked people was the sudden loss of weight after my divorce losing 33 lbs. I had just decided to fight harder for my life like I wasn't already giving it all I had. I just didn't want to end up with health problems and suffer the way that my parents had. Their deaths were so traumatic to me that I still have 6-month check-ups for everything to make sure anything would be caught in the early stages.

A friend asked me to her party once and said, "I have my photographer coming to my party, and I asked him to take your pictures". I was shocked and didn't understand why she was doing that. She is much younger than me and lives near NYC. She's gorgeous, and she does this and just wanted me to feel good about myself, I guess, after everything I have been through. This was at the same time that I had a possible project that was in motion but sadly did not come to fruition. However, the shock factor was already out there, so I decided to roll with it. There was a lot of judgment passed as I did what I could to trudge forward and navigate divorce, single motherhood, and running a home financially myself. I've already spoken about so many that stepped in to help me heal and become the still-developing version of myself that I am today. It's times like this when your friend Erin reads what you've written, knowing your story as it was developing all along and still stating that she was amazed. That you, my spiritual and real-life friend, for your presence in my life.

I'd love to chat about my beautiful fluffy-haired friend that, in my opinion, is a direct angel from heaven. This friend, with so many overlapping experiences, literally held my hand and guided me to every single healer (medical professional) that are the best in the area, and she was never wrong. Not only that, but she is one of the most supportive family members that I have ever met. She and her entire family are just nothing short of amazing. I actually love them all so much. They were there for me as a collective group when I didn't have anyone around. They didn't just do it to do it, either. It was out of mutual respect and care. Her parents came to my home and helped me clean the house really well after my divorce. Her mother helped argue with me and reorganize. I laughed at the experience but needed a "stand-in" Mom to tell me that it was okay to get rid of certain things. She knew where I was coming from and would have free reign to tell me, "No, Keli". This is a friendship that, for certain, could only have come from God. These sisters and their families are just the light. I love them, and I can truly say they were one of the reasons that I could pick myself back up and keep fighting. They're excellent role models, and this just goes to show purpose and intent on who you have surrounding you during healing times.

The second round of photos came from an opportunity to join a challenge called The 40 over 40 Portrait Project by photographer Angelique at Eye Spy Studio. That's when the imaginative part of me came to life with Angelique's amazing photography talent. The angel photos and such had emerged. It was met with a 50/50 reaction of "are you a model", and I laughed, answering, "Nope," to "does she think she's truly an angel"? The answer is yes. I absolutely think I am an Earth Angel who dedicates her life and everything she has been through as a way to help show others how to navigate these difficulties and come back to the light. Openly an "Omnist" who celebrates God, Jesus, Mother Mary, Archangels, Angels, Ascended Masters, Ancestors, and spirit guides. I work closely and lovingly with children and animals.

I have become part of round 2 of the 40 over 40 projects because it was so freeing. Angelique helped me channel another level of healing by taking a version of what we first created, adding to it with more imagination than ever with the opposing white dress angel and red dress woman reaching for help. The best part is that she took a trauma that existed when my psychologist called me a wild black beauty when I broke into PTSD about what my permanent damage would be after the accident or how long it would take to heal and turned it into what my friends have now called "black stallion photo shoot like top model Keli Kane". My peeps are funny. I can seriously say I don't know who would have been able to pull that off, from the coordination of the make-up artist to the prepping of that gorgeous horse, to the pictures during frigid weather, and no one was the wiser except for us.

It was connections through my friend Patti and University Magickus that had me meet Peter Beddard, who in turn helped me to meet the beautiful Jacquie Jordan and Stephanie Cobian. I then became part of TVGUESTPERT doing motivational speaking in healing traumas through podcasts. I even participated in an online journal in regards to what teaching during the pandemic looked like. It's been such an honor just learning from Jacquie and Stephanie. I have been sharing the idea to tell my story for a while now and I finally got it done. My sister also trapped me in a long car ride recently and told me it was time to stop procrastinating and get the job done. My sister knows that this is part of my healing journey. She meant nothing other than wrap this up sister and heal. So highly motivated by my Sis I wrote the book in 2 months while holding my regular working schedule. It was just time and the information poured out of me. I also just completed the trip to CA visiting Patti, Merle, Cristina, Kristi, and my agent Stephanie Cobian. I got to meet her adorable son and I tell you with all of my heart I have finally ended this chapter of traumas. I'm finally feeling like I'm balanced and back where I need to be. I've created an even stronger version of myself completely healed. This trip was so enlightening and has given me the opportunity to move forward and live life to the fullest.

The people who I had read this before coming out said to me, "I know you and you're story, and you still shocked me". That's because I love love. I love being happy whenever I can be, and however I can be, I try. I live for love. I hope I'm sharing that love with you all now. Please be well on your journey. Love & Light to you ALL! "

Made in the USA
Columbia, SC
07 April 2023

49ed30b9-8984-4c7a-b125-2fc14b522684R01

DEFINE YOU

A 40-Day Biblical Challenge to Claim and Manifest Your God-Given Destiny!

Scripture Quotations

Published by

Chris Noble Christian Life Coaching

www.ChrisNobleCLC.com

ISBN: 979-8-89525-438-7

Printed in the United States of America